THE PROPHET AND THE REVOLUTIONARY

THE PROPHET AND THE REVOLUTIONARY

ARAB

SOCIALISM

IN

THE

MODERN

MIDDLE

EAST

BY STEPHEN GOODE

Franklin Watts, Inc.   New York   1975

Library of Congress Cataloging in Publication Data
Goode, Stephen.
    The prophet and the revolutionary.
    SUMMARY: Traces the rise of radical socialism
in Egypt, Iraq, Algeria, and Syria discussing the historical reasons for its development, its successes and
failures, and its effect on the rest of the Arab world.
    1. Socialism in Arab countries—Case studies—
Juvenile literature. 2. Arab countries—Politics and
government—Case studies—Juvenile literature.
[1. Arab countries—Politics and government]
I. Title.
HX434.A6G66   335'.00917'4927   75–6816
ISBN 0-531-02840-2

For my grandmother,
Ethel Vanscoy

TABLE OF CONTENTS

INTRODUCTION

This is a book about radical politics and government in four Arab nations. Egypt, Algeria, Syria, and Iraq have all undergone revolutions in the past twenty years, which have altered the traditional social and economic patterns that had existed for centuries. Socialism, in various forms, has made its appearance in these countries, and each has emerged as a nation of some importance and significance in the modern world.

When discussing these nations, the average Westerner displays a lack of knowledge and awareness that is unfortunate. He tends to lump all the Arab nations together and to see them as reflecting identical customs, language, and tradition. Yet the North African nation of Algeria is as different from Middle Eastern Iraq as Guatemala is from Canada, or Spain from Sweden. Algerians cannot comprehend the Arabic spoken by the average Iraqi, and the problems faced by the North African are different from those faced in the Middle East. It is true that all four nations discussed at length in this book are Islamic, and, to varying degrees, Arab, but history and geography have combined to make each country individual, and each people distinct from another. Most Arabs are Muslims, that is, followers of Mohammad, but there is a significant Christian minority throughout the Middle East. It is hoped, therefore, that the reader will gain some knowledge of the diversity and complexity of the Arab World.

There has been much romance attached to the revolutionaries that have transformed so much of the Arab World. Once when this author was sitting in front of the Academy of Art in Vienna, a young Austrian approached him and reverently asked him if he were an Arab. When the author replied, no, he wasn't, he was an American, the change in attitude on the part of the Austrian was marked. He moved indignantly away, frowning and disgusted, and soon began tossing pebbles in derision and ridicule. Instantly, the object of his inquiry had turned from a respected symbol of rebellion and revolution into the arch-symbol of imperialism and oppression. Upon examination, however, this young Austrian student proved ignorant of the problems and the achievements experienced by the Arab radicals he admired, and was more willing to admire them from afar than to look into their day-to-day problems and solutions. In America, too, people of the left or the right have been willing to praise or condemn the Arab radicals without any close analysis of what it was and is the Arab radicals have been trying to create. The second and final purpose of this book, therefore, is to examine objectively the goals and accomplishments, the successes and failures, of radical Arab politics. It is hoped thereby that the majority of radical Arab leaders will emerge as neither superhuman heroes, transforming their world through superior knowledge or morality, nor as vicious monsters bent on destroying all that is good and sacred, but as men who have attempted to alleviate the age-old poverty and ignorance of their countries.

Problems of space have precluded a discussion of the whole Arab World. The conservative monarchies, such as Morocco, Jordan, and Saudi Arabia, are not discussed. Tunisia, a moderate nation that has undertaken much socialist reform, is likewise omitted because it has never joined the more radical and dramatic nations more commonly associated with what is known as Arab Socialism. Four other nations —the two Yemens, the Sudan, and Libya—have undergone revolutions and claim membership among the radicals, but are avoided here because their revolutions have been too recent for assessment or because they are so backward that revolution has no meaning in their context. The reader will learn of these other Arab countries only as they relate to the four radical Arab states.

Egypt, Algeria, Syria, and Iraq are therefore the subject of this book. Of the four, only Syria and Iraq are unqualifiedly Arab nations.

Egypt and Algeria have often been excluded by purists who claim their tradition and history are too diverse and varied to be truly Arab. Yet both the Egyptian and Algerian revolutionaries have claimed intimate connection with an Arab past and have wanted to create a union of all Arab nations. For this reason, they are included in this book among the Arab countries.

CHAPTER ONE

The Arab World Today

Only a generation ago, most people thought of the Arab World as an area of deserts, camels, and robed sheikhs who warred on one another over ancient feuds. The Arabs played no significant part in world affairs, and if an educated Westerner knew something of that part of the world, it was that ancient civilizations had once thrived there. The ruins of Babylon, the pyramids of Egypt, and the other archeological finds of French, English, and American scientists were widely discussed and familiar to every schoolboy, but about current affairs next to nothing was known. The Arabs were considered a backward, ignorant people, and it was hoped that they would improve themselves and learn civilized government from the European officials who governed them.

In a few years, this conception has altered. The Middle East has emerged as one of the most important and widely discussed areas in world affairs. The Arabs have become a dynamic people, challenging world order and demanding to be seen and heard. This extraordinary change can be attributed to three factors: the discovery of vast oil reserves under the barren desert sands, the establishment of the Jewish State in Palestine, a move that Arabs took as a deep insult to their pride and dignity, and the development of a new, vital political ideology among the Arabs, the ideology that has come to be known as Arab Socialism.

The discovery of oil has had an extraordinary effect on the Middle East. The world's largest and richest supplies of oil were found in areas that had once been considered worthless and where it was impossible to grow and raise even the barest necessities of life. Geologists now estimate that from 60 to 75 percent of the world's known oil reserves are under Arab soil. In a world increasingly dependent on oil for its industry, transportation, and technology, the possession of so much oil inevitably gives the Arab World enormous political power and economic leverage. Europe alone depends on the Middle East for 85 percent of her oil needs, and Japan, with no supply of her own, must depend entirely on the world market. The United States has been more fortunate than Japan or Europe and fills most of her requirements from other sources. Yet recent estimates show that even America will depend more and more in the future on the oil the Arab states can supply.

In recent years the Arabs have profited enormously from their most valuable resource. Only five years ago, income from oil in the Middle East was only $4.5 billion. Now that income has greatly increased, and Iraq alone enjoyed a profit of $5 billion last year. It is estimated that by 1980 the yearly income for the whole Arab World will have reached $40 billion or more, an income equal to that of the five hundred largest corporations in the United States. The Arab nations will drain the gold supplies of the formerly wealthy, industrialized West, and much of the economic power that has been concentrated in the United States and Europe could find itself in Arab hands. Already Arabs are investing in American and European enterprises, and some observers expect them to purchase large hotel and motel chains in the United States and to buy controlling interests in European and American television networks and newspapers. Such investments will help them to sway Western public opinion and exert influence on decisions made concerning the Middle East. For the average Arab, too, the discovery of great wealth has made a difference. The citizen of oil-rich Libya, only a decade ago a poor nation, now enjoys an average income of $4,000, while the citizen of the Sheikhdom of Kuwait boasts a comparable income that is coupled with social and welfare aid that takes care of him from birth until death. Clearly, Allah has smiled on the Arab lands.

The second factor that has brought the Arab World so dramati-

cally to the center of world affairs is the continuing conflict with
Israel. After World War II, Great Britain, the United States, and the
Soviet Union were responsible for the establishment of a Jewish State
in the Arab province of Palestine. It was argued with reason and
humanity that the Jews who had survived Hitler's concentration
camps and executions needed a homeland where they would never
again fall victim to a vicious anti-Semitism.

Thousands of Jews had already settled in Palestine before World
War II, but the creation of a Jewish State was nevertheless taken as a
deep insult by the Arabs. The Arabs pointed to the fact that thousands of Palestinian Arabs who had lived in Palestine for centuries
would be forced from their land and that those Arabs who might
choose to remain would be second-class citizens in a state that did
not share their religion or tradition. Likewise, the Arab World saw
the establishment of Israel as a challenge to their independence and
freedom. The Arab nations had been struggling against European
domination for decades, and it appeared to them that Israel was
merely another Western maneuver to maintain a foothold in the
Middle East and preserve control over Arab affairs.

From the moment of Israel's creation, Arab extremists have
urged a war to drive the Israelis "into the sea." Moderate Arab voices
that have hoped for some compromise and accommodation with the
Jewish State have been pushed aside and largely discredited. The Israelis have made it clear that they will stay in their new home, while
the Arabs have made it equally clear that they hope someday to
achieve redress for the suffering and insult they feel they have
endured. Four bloody Arab-Israeli wars have been fought since 1948,
and the whole world has been drawn into the controversy. American
policy has guaranteed the existence of Israel and has supplied weapons, airplanes, and ammunition, while the Soviet Union, with its long
desire to establish a foothold of influence and power in the Middle
East, has done the same for the Arab nations. Indeed, the Middle
East has become a center of the Cold War conflict, and the President
of the United States has called it the greatest existing threat to world
peace. Throughout the world, newspapers are filled with what hap-
pens from day to day in the Arab World, and people are hopeful that
a war will not break out that will bring the great superpowers, America and Russia, into war with one another.

Recently, the Arab nations combined their status as oil-rich countries with their desire to see the power of Israel limited. After the fourth Arab-Israeli War of October 1973, Arab countries, conservative and radical alike, declared an oil boycott of Europe and the United States. They hoped that the boycott would bring the Western nations around to a policy that was less pro-Israel and more pro-Arab. As the boycott took effect, gasoline and other fuels began to disappear; long lines of cars appeared at filling stations in America and Europe, the price on all kinds of fuel skyrocketed. In the Netherlands, a country adamantly pro-Israel, people began to ride bicycles and to look for alternatives that did not make them dependent on oil.

Whether the boycott was effective is not yet clear. But by the summer of 1974 a whole new relationship had developed between the West and the Arab nations. In a series of exhausting and brilliant negotiations, the American secretary of state, Henry Kissinger, had altered much that was taken for granted in the Middle East. The oil boycott was lifted, and Israel withdrew from the territory it had occupied during the October War. But most amazingly, the radical Arab nations of Syria and Egypt had begun to talk with the United States and to settle differences with the West and with Israel. Richard Nixon, the American President, visited Cairo and Damascus, Amman, Jordan, and Saudi Arabia. The American government promised nuclear reactors to Egypt, as well as other economic aid. A new situation had been created in the Middle East. Skeptics argued that the situation of two decades could not be altered overnight, that the settlement was tenuous and could erupt at any moment in another war. Yet it was clear that Nixon and Kissinger had counterbalanced the Soviet influence in the Arab World and had reestablished American prestige in Egypt and elsewhere. Only time would tell if this new balance would be destroyed and if the old battle lines would be redrawn. Meanwhile, President Sadat and other Arab leaders could boast that they had successfully negotiated an agreement favorable to the Arabs with nations that had long supported Israel and opposed Arab interests. Arab power and prestige had risen to new heights.

Finally, a third factor that has changed the Middle East and brought it to the attention of the whole world is the emergence of a radical political philosophy that has caught the allegiance of many Arabs. Before Nasser, no Arab leader had won the imagination and respect of large numbers of Arabs or had gained the notice of people throughout the world. Arab affairs had seemed only of local interest, and no Arab leader seemed capable of freeing himself and his people from links with the European powers.

But Nasser changed all that. He and his followers overthrew the corrupt Egyptian monarchy of King Farouk and established a new government that evolved into the first Arab Socialist state. For Nasser, the crisis that faced the Arab World—its backwardness and poverty, its weakness and ignorance—could no longer be tolerated— he wanted to do something about it. In Egypt, he began the disruption of the old system that had favored the rich and powerful; land was seized and turned over to peasants who had formerly owned nothing. Other social and economic measures were undertaken to improve the condition of the masses. Abroad, Nasser announced that Egypt would follow the orders of no one. He drove the British completely out of Egypt and gained headlines throughout the world as he successfully thwarted the attempts of Britain and France to exert control over Egyptian affairs. Along with Tito of Yugoslavia and Nehru of India, Nasser became a leader of the Third World. His example gave hope and courage to dependent and backward nations that they too could overthrow their colonial masters and establish a new order. Young idealists in Arab lands and elsewhere envisioned themselves as new Nassers and studied the work of the Egyptian leader and his followers, hoping to imitate his rise to power and his reforms in Egypt.

Seldom does one man exert so much influence on history. Often roundly condemned for his egregious errors and miscalculations, Nasser nevertheless had shown that it might be done, that change might be accomplished; he had shown what natural talent, hard work, and dedication might accomplish. After Nasser's coup d'état, revolution came to Algeria, Iraq, Syria, and elsewhere in the Arab World, and although these other revolutionary leaders might disclaim any connection with Nasser and profess no admiration for the Egyptian leader, they nevertheless owed him much. A new aggressive spirit had established itself in the Middle East that altered the cautious and passive attitudes of the conservative Arab states, causing them to proclaim their Arabism more loudly; this new aggressive spirit likewise forced America and Russia to take notice of the new order in that part of the world. Egypt, Algeria, Syria, and Iraq were no longer pliable and predictable; they were now independent nations to be reckoned with seriously.

The revolutions that have come to the Arab nations have helped to focus world attention on the Arabs. The four radical nations have been the most vociferous opponents of Israel, announcing time and time again that they were dedicated to total war against the Zionist state. It was in the radical Arab states that the Soviet Union first made its inroads into the Middle East, toppling the balance of power there and challenging world stability. Indeed, the Russians came at the invitation of radical Arabs who sought to use the communists and communist aid in the struggle against Israel and the West. Likewise, it has been the radical states that have taken the initiative in organizing the oil boycott against the West; the boycott would not have worked without the support of King Faisal, but it was the radicals who goaded the king on and convinced him that the boycott should be made.

Arab radicalism has taken different forms in the four different countries where it has seized power. In each country it refers to itself as socialist, but it is a peculiar type of socialism that Western socialists often have difficulty in identifying. Arab Socialism has found its most ardent supporters among young army officers. Never in the West has a leftist socialist movement worked through the army to gain control of a government. Likewise, Arab Socialism seems most concerned with the peasant, who makes up the vast majority of Arab society, rather than with the industrial worker, who has been traditionally the primary concern of Western socialism.

But the most glaring distinction between Arab Socialism and Western socialism has been the strong and vigorous element of nationalism that has existed in Arab Socialism from its conception. Indeed, the most noticeable and impelling characteristic of Arab Socialism has been nationalism, for above all else, the radicals of the Middle East have been concerned with the revival of Arab dignity and strength, with the establishment of national unity and purpose. Socialism in the West, on the other hand, has usually sought to play down nationalism, arguing that nationalism is a doctrine that leads to wars between nations over problems that really do not concern the vast majority of citizens. Western socialists have been suspicious of nationalism, for they feel it is an ideology used by conservative and reactionary governments to avoid social and economic change. Most sophisticated Western socialists believe that nationalism is an artificial concept no longer needed, a concept that deludes the worker into believing that his interests lie totally with those of the nation as a whole, when, in truth, his interests lie with social and economic improvement and not with national pride.

Arab nationalism first appeared as a cohesive and growing movement in the early part of the twentieth century. It sought independence for the Arabs first from the Turks, who had ruled the Middle East for centuries, and then from Britain and France, who had taken over when the Turkish Empire crumbled. The struggle against foreign occupation was protracted and often vicious; the Arabs, politically immature and inexperienced after centuries of foreign domination, had to search for a political system that would give them the strength and vitality they wanted. Monarchy, democracy, fascism, and other forms were experimented with and rejected as inadequate or too slow. Arab Socialism has appeared as one of the ideologies linked to the nationalist drive for independence, power, and self-respect. Unlike the West, where nationalism and socialism appeared as movements in different periods of history, in the Middle East nationalism and socialism have almost grown up together, reinforcing one another and borrowing one another's ideas and methods.

But if Western socialists find much that is different in Arab Socialism—in its military origins, its concern for the peasant, and in its nationalism—they also find much that reminds them of their own socialist traditions. There is the desire to improve the condition of the underdog and to limit the power and influence of the wealthy and privileged. There is the desire to follow a course of government planning to achieve economic and social improvement and social justice. Indeed, the element of European socialism most wholeheartedly adopted into Arab Socialism has been the idea of closely guided social planning under the auspices of an authoritarian government. Many Arab Socialists have expressed admiration for the Soviet Union and its impressive achievement of turning a backward and weak nation into a major world power in less than fifty years. They hope to gain the same success in an even shorter period of time. Arab Socialists are impatient, and they want the shortest possible means to attain their goals of nationalism coupled with economic and social change.

When one looks at the state of the Arab World today, it is easy to understand the urgency Arab radicals feel. Political and economic events have thrust the Middle East into the center of world affairs, but poverty, disease, and other forms of human misery remain part of everyday life. International significance and oil wealth have not brought prosperity and improvement to all Arabs; indeed, many live under the same conditions of ignorance and backwardness that have been part of Arab life for centuries. Arab Socialism, during the short period of its existence, has begun the attack on these conditions, but has had to work against difficult odds. The Arab World today is a society in transition; one where expectations for the future are hopeful, but where the social and economic inheritance still hinders true progress and where the majority of people experience little of the abundance and ease enjoyed by the people of Europe or America.

Perhaps the most immediate and obvious problem has been that of social structure. At the top of traditional Arab society has been a small number of sheikhs, merchants, landowners, and other notables who controlled what wealth, land, and power the Arab World had to offer. These rich and powerful individuals formed only a small percentage of the population, and an enormous gulf separated them from other Arabs. No middle class of any size, composed of small-business men, government officials, or other professional people, ever developed as it had in Europe or America, where the middle class opposed the power of the aristocracy and formed the backbone of the democratic and liberal tradition.

The vast majority of Arabs have been farmers who live in the villages that dot the Nile, the Tigris and Euphrates, and the Mediterranean coastline of Algeria. Most have had very small plots of land that yield barely enough to survive or own no land at all. In Egypt, for centuries, the peasants have lived below subsistence level, unable to give their families the food and housing they need. In Algeria, Syria, and Iraq, their level of existence has been somewhat higher, but still perilously near subsistence level, sometimes drifting above it, sometimes below it.

The plight of the Middle Eastern farmer has been aggravated by other circumstances. Islam, the religion of the majority of people, does not place much value on the land or on those who work it. It has rather been a religion of the nomadic Bedouins who live in the desert or of the merchants and others of the cities. The peasants live in a world that places little value on their lives, a world that has not been moved to alleviate their condition until very recently.

Geographic circumstance, too, has been against the Arab peasant. Since most of the Middle East and North Africa is desert or land otherwise unfit for crops, there is only one-tenth of the area that can be cultivated. Already, two-thirds of the cultivatable land has been placed in use, so there is not much room for expansion. Except for the cotton crop in Syria, most of the land yields a low product, so that the peasant finds his work rewarded by a small return compared to the return per acre received in Europe or America. Ignorance of modern agriculture likewise condemns the peasant farmer to poverty and inefficiency. But even where modern techniques and knowledge are available, poverty prevents widespread use of new machinery, fertilizer, or insecticides.

Laws of inheritance have traditionally played against the peasant, for land was distributed among all the sons of the family. In societies where men are permitted up to four wives at one time, this has often meant severe fragmentation of property, so that sons or grandsons received far too little to live on. Many were forced to become day laborers, being paid very little and owning no property or land. This system condemned many to poverty and starvation and made it impossible for the Arab nations to grow enough food to feed their people adequately.

The extreme poverty of the peasants forced them to borrow money so that they could buy the seeds and tools they needed to work the land. Often they borrowed this money from moneylenders who charged as much as 100 percent interest, forcing the peasants into perpetual debt. Studies done on the farming villages of Egypt before the advent of Arab Socialism show that the majority of the farmers owed large sums, which they were unable to pay.

Traditionally, too, the peasant carried the chief tax load in the nation, paying a tax far higher than he could afford and living in fear of the government that seemed to bother him only when it needed money. This heavy tax burden was in marked contrast to the relatively light taxes levied on the wealthy, absentee landowners who lived in the cities and enjoyed luxurious vacations in Europe. The end result of this unjust social system was the creation of a large number of poverty-stricken, underfed, and uneducated people who were tied to the land and who, to this day, do not have the background, training, or opportunity to find other work or improve their condition. This population forms the chief social and economic problem facing the radical Arab governments, and it will be some time before the rural poor are raised to a level where genuine progress and improvement can take place.

The poor of the cities—Cairo, Algiers, Alexandria, Damascus, and Baghdad—fare little better than the villagers. The low level of industrial development has created few jobs in factories, and most urban Arabs work in positions connected with commerce, tourism, handicraft manufacture or government administration. Most of these jobs are low-paying, and a sizable portion of the city population remains out of work and unemployable. Even where industrialization has taken place, as with the oil industry in Iraq, the number of poorer Arabs affected remains small. Many Arab governments have feared the labor movement and have outlawed the establishment of labor unions or other organizations that might have improved the lot of the worker.

Besides poverty, disease has been a besetting factor of Arab life. Up through the late nineteenth century, plague periodically wiped out large numbers of people. Some headway was made against this, but to this day, many Arabs fall victim to diseases that have long since disappeared from Europe or America. Beginning in 1948, for instance, a team of Egyptian and American doctors studied several Egyptian villages over a period of four years. They found that half the people were infected with lice and three-quarters had fleas. Ninety percent had trachoma, a disease of the eyes, and one out of every twelve villagers was blind in one or both eyes. Ninety-five percent of the males of all ages had bilharziasis, which is caused by a parasite that enters the body and attacks organs such as the bladder. There is likewise a high rate of infant mortality resulting from the lack of trained midwives or doctors and an ignorance of modern sanitation and health care. Reports have shown that such diseases are more common in Egypt, where the population is dense, than in the rest of the Arab World, but no Middle Eastern country is free of pain and suffering that could be eradicated if modern medical science were available to all.

The Middle East and North Africa are likewise plagued with one of the highest birthrates in the world. In an area already perplexed by low crop output and a scarce supply of land, population grows by leaps and bounds. This condition is especially found in Egypt, the largest of the Arab countries in population, where the people are crowded along the banks of the Nile, the only part of the country capable of supporting life. But Algeria, Syria, and Iraq, as well as the Arab countries under conservative governments, have a rapid population growth that has been enhanced by successes made against the plague and infant mortality. The census data coming from the Middle East are unreliable and exact figures cannot be given, but most observers agree that city and countryside alike have been affected by the growth, the villages becoming more thickly populated and the cities expanding rapidly as thousands leave the rural areas to find livelihood in the cities. Housing has become a severe problem, and no Arab nation has proved capable of providing the number of new apartments and homes necessary to house the expanding population.

The standard of living in the Middle East is also affected by the general ignorance of the population. Most males are illiterate, or, if literate, know little else than the Koran and other religious works. Women have traditionally been kept in a state of near servitude, prevented from all self-expression, and told that their duties involved the care of children and the running of the household. The Koran repeatedly describes woman as "one step below man," and, until recently, women have had few rights or opportunities. Because of the low educational level of both men and women, it has been impossible for Arab countries to find people capable of administering an efficient government or of utilizing modern technology.

A final element of modern Arab life that has contributed to the crisis is change itself. Because of modernization and the influence of modern technology, thousands of Arabs feel displaced and find themselves in a no-man's-land between the old and the new. This era of difficult transition is superficially expressed in clothing, as more and more young Arabs have chosen to wear Western type dress, abandoning the traditional Arab robes. Even the most vehement Arab nationalist, such as Qaddafi of Libya, is seen more often in Western military uniform or fatigues than in traditional garb. Western furniture too is popular, and more and more Arab homes are supplied with chairs, tables, and lamps that make them hard to distinguish from houses in Europe or America.

This transition from old to new is also expressed in the building of new cities and the destruction of the old sections that have stood for centuries. This change was noticed by the great English novelist E. M. Forster, who lived for some time in Alexandria and wrote a book about the city's architecture and history. When he returned to Alexandria several years later, Forster was shocked and dismayed by the number of buildings that he had loved which had been torn down and replaced by less attractive modern buildings. Often it seems as though the Arabs are more anxious to destroy or hide, instead of protect and preserve, the heritage they claim to want to revive and renew.

Change and modernization have contributed to the destruction of traditional Arab family ties, which have played an important part in Arab society. No longer does the young Arab feel close to his father; other loyalties have come to his attention: where can he find a job? how can he acquire the education and skills necessary for the modern world? what political ideology best answers the needs of his country? These are questions his father cannot answer. New freedom for women has likewise caused the old family relationships to dissolve, and more and more, especially in the cities, the father is not held to be the infallible head of the family.

The decline in family and kinship solidarity has been followed by a decline in localism. Earlier, Arabs identified themselves with the region they and their relatives were from and felt no sense of national unity or of union with other Arabs throughout the Middle East. Now, as Arab governments centralize authority and attempt to consolidate tribes and regions into modern states, new loyalties develop, and the old localism becomes isolating and limiting. Even many of the Bedouins, the most fiercely individual and traditional of Arab groups, have been forced to settle down. In Iraq they have been hired as workers in the oil industry and have abandoned their nomadic existence. Indeed, the old folk culture, with its tribal and local characteristics, has been dying all over the Arab World, to be replaced by modern mass communication. Radio, television, and newspapers have made Arabs aware of the outside world and have focused attention away from older religious and social concerns. A generation gap of considerable proportions has developed between an older generation that relied on the Koran for every answer to life's problems and a younger, more sophisticated generation that must find answers to problems the Koran did not anticipate.

This secularization of attitude has been perhaps the single most amazing alteration in the Arab World, for it has meant a major abandonment of the past. As in the West, science and reason are winning the struggle against conservative religion and tradition. Daniel Lerner, an able American sociologist who has written extensively on the Middle East, has described this new attitude as one of "Mecca vs. mechanization," or of the confrontation of Islam, of which Mecca is the Holy City, with the process of modernization and mechanization of everyday life. Where modern machinery and technology are introduced, great change cannot be far behind. Indeed, the process of mechanization has gone far, for the pilgrimage to Mecca, one of the duties of the devout Muslim, once done on foot and camelback, is now done by automobile and other forms of modern transportation.

Secularization has been a long time in coming to the Middle East, and it is far from complete. It took the West centuries to develop a modern attitude toward life, one governed by a rational and scientific view of the world, and it will take the Arab World some time to overcome the traditions and attitudes of centuries. But where secularism has come, in the cities and among a sizable portion of the young, educated Muslims, it has so undermined the past and discredited it that it has added to the tension created by backwardness and poverty and has been one of the forces shaping the crisis in the Arab World.

The crisis of the Arab World is thus one of rising hopes and expectations for a better future in the face of extreme poverty, ignorance, and backwardness. A vicious, self-defeating circle has developed as many Arabs, demanding rapid transition to modern civilization, are condemned to slow, uneven change because of the very age-old poverty and ignorance they want to change. Time was when the Arab looked forward to a happy afterlife in the heaven promised by Allah, where the believer would rest on hammocks in a beautiful oasis and be waited on by lovely servant girls. Now the Arab would rather change the present world and make it more comfortable, livable, and pleasant.

Arab Socialism has been one philosophy developed to answer the growing social, economic, and political problems facing the Arab World. It has not been the only reaction to the dilemma. Some Arab governments have remained conservative, choosing to modernize slowly under the supervision of a traditional monarchy. Others have sought moderate change under the rule of a strong man. But Arab Socialism now, in its various forms, the political philosophy of Iraq, Syria, Egypt, and Algeria—nations that encompass more than half the population of the Arab World—is clearly the most visible and dramatic of the various Arab ideologies. Of the three factors that have changed the Middle East—the discovery of oil, the creation of Israel, and the development of Arab Socialism—Arab Socialism remains the most elusive and difficult to understand. It is now time to look closely at the Arab World, to survey its history and to see how socialism appeared as one answer to the crisis that threatened to destroy the Arab World in the twentieth century.

CHAPTER TWO

The Historical Roots of the Crisis

The greatest single factor in the decline and stagnation of the Arab World has been the weight of history itself. Centuries of misrule and political apathy have left their mark on the Middle East, and one of the great tasks facing the Arabs today is the clearing away of the debris and wreckage of the past. One of the remarkable characteristics of European and American civilization has been the relative ease with which alteration and revolution have taken place within society, making change and transition so much a part of our lives that we hardly notice them. With other civilizations, however, it has not been so. Indian and Chinese culture became frozen in caste and social systems that impeded change for hundreds of years. Likewise, Arab society developed traditions and institutions that not only resisted alteration, but condemned it as evil and unholy. To understand the crisis in the modern Arab World, therefore, it is necessary to survey Arab history and observe those elements that have contributed to social indifference and backwardness. Occasionally, those characteristics that have given Arab society vitality and strength will be found, but more often those characteristics that act as hindrances and obstacles to progress will be discovered. It is these hindrances that radical Arab governments want to eliminate and erase from Arab life.

Arab society was molded thirteen hundred years ago during the time of the Prophet Mohammad, the man who established the values and traditions long held sacred by most Arabs. To be sure, the

Middle East and North Africa had been the home of older civilizations. In the area today called Syria and Iraq, Sumerians and Akkadians, Assyrians and Babylonians had raised empires. At the time of Mohammad, Egypt had a recorded history going back three thousand years, and, in the first century B.C. the armies of Rome had entered the area, beginning to bring all of North Africa and much of the Middle East under Rome's control. But most of these ancient empires had disappeared by the time of Mohammad, and even Rome, the greatest of them all, was in decline. It was in this period of decline that the Arabs appeared and became the next great empire builders.

In the seventh century, the Arabs were a people living in what is now called the Arabian Peninsula. They had been primarily a desert people, but by the time of Mohammad, many had settled in cities and had taken up trade and commerce. They were undergoing a transition from their earlier nomadic customs to the urban traditions necessary for the thriving trade they carried on in their growing cities. Just as it is today, Arab society was experiencing a crisis between old and new. Many older Arabs rejected the settled life that came with trade and wealth and thought that the old ways, the warrior virtues of courage and strength, were best. Younger Arabs, however, felt that the old ways hampered progress and that some way had to be found to make room for the new. Commerce and cities were here to stay, they must have argued, and it was best to accept them and learn to live with them.

In this crisis, an exceptionally able man came forth to give unity and stability to Arab life. This was Mohammad, who was born about 570 in the city of Mecca, one of the thriving commercial cities of the Arabian Peninsula. As a young man, Mohammad worked for a rich widow who owned caravans that traveled to various parts of the Middle East. He proved a successful merchant, and soon became respected for his honesty and his business ability. He married the widow, who was several years older than he was, and soon he was established as one of the principal businessmen of Mecca.

But Mohammad was not an average merchant, and during retreats he made to the desert regions around Mecca, he began to have visions. These visions soon convinced him that he had been chosen by God to reform Arab society and establish a new order that would turn Arabs back to their original God and their early religious values. He began to preach to his fellow Meccans about his visions, and, at first, he was considered eccentric and harmless. But soon his attacks on contemporary Arab society grew strong and dangerous. Former friends and business associates began to harass and vilify him. People refused to speak to him or to pay debts they owed him. Finally, Mohammad and the few believers he had converted were forced to flee to Medina, another Arab city at some distance from Mecca. He had been invited to Medina by its citizens, who hoped that he could settle the tribal disputes that were tearing the city apart. It was in Medina that Mohammad's faith, which has come to be known as Islam, was first accepted wholeheartedly. The year of Mohammad's flight from Mecca to his new home, 622, became the year one of the Islamic faith.

Mohammad settled the disputes that had raged between the people of Medina. He brought order and stability to the city and soon began to spread his faith into the surrounding area. He formed an army that he led into battle against his opponents. When he defeated the enemy at the famous battle of Badr, against odds that seemed insurmountable, his reputation spread far and wide, for many Arabs valued courage and military ability above all else. Mohammad's success seemed to prove that God was indeed on his side.

By the time he died in 632, Mohammad had organized the whole peninsula and had brought even the Meccans to his side. He governed personally and heard the grievances of all, emphasizing the need for peaceful settlement of conflict. One of his chief warnings to his fellow Arabs was that they would never be great or receive the favor of God if they continued to war among themselves. Mohammad gave the Arab people the example of a simple, moderate life, for he did not drink, nor indulge in excesses of any kind. He had not been a violent man, and urged his followers to treat others decently and fairly. He had always used his army to create order and stability, not as a means of pure aggression. He likewise set a new standard for behavior toward women; while not allowing them total equality with men, he nevertheless raised them from their former status of near servitude. Mohammad took only one wife while his first, the rich widow, was alive, and he honored and respected her. Even after her death, he limited the number of his wives to four, the number he said he could best support, and made it part of his new faith that all his followers do likewise. Mohammad's genius had established stability and unity for the first time in Arab history and had left the Arabs with a religion and a set of beliefs that were to give order and purpose to Arab society to the present day.

The faith that Mohammad established reflects the simplicity and concerns of its founder whose visions were collected and written down in the Koran, the Holy Book of Islam. The faith required only five major duties of the believer, but it did elaborate a complete guide for the daily life of every Muslim, a guide so complete that it included descriptions of the food a believer cannot eat, the manner in which he was to wash his beard, the musical instruments he could play, and the answer to many other problems that might arise in day-to-day life. One of the outstanding features of Islam was that it offered a meaningful pattern for life to a people moving from tribal society to the more complex life of cities. Throughout its history, Islam has continued to appeal to such people and is to this day making converts among Africans who, having found their old ways destroyed, are in search of a guide to help them in their dilemma.

The five basic duties that Mohammad commanded his followers to perform began with the acknowledgment that there was only one God and that his name was Allah. Allah was all-powerful and had created all things. Mohammad was his last and greatest Prophet, for the Koran taught that Moses, Jesus, and the other great teachers of the Bible were also important, but that Mohammad fulfilled and perfected their prophecy. Next, the Muslim was told to pray five times daily to Allah and to recognize his total dependence on Allah's Will. Third, he was to fast during the month of Rahmadan, the month of Mohammad's flight from Mecca to Medina, and, fourth, to make a pilgrimage to Mecca at least once in his lifetime. The final duty was that each of the faithful give alms to support the poor and needy, for Muslims were to take care of their destitute and have compassion for the unfortunate. A sixth function of the Muslim was mentioned in the Koran but was not raised in importance to the status of the first five. This was the concept of Holy War, or Jihad, that reflected Mohammad's own role as a military leader. Holy War was to be conducted against pagans to bring them into the faith, but it was not to be directed against Christians and Jews, who were "peoples of the Book," that is, the Bible, who believed many of the same things held sacred by Muslims.

The Koran not only elaborated a code for the daily lives of the faithful but went on to make suggestions about government and about social and economic problems that have influenced Arab thinking and practice for centuries. One of the clearest social and political opinions to emerge was the emphasis on equality. Time and time again, the Scripture reminded the believer that everything on the earth belongs to Allah. Nothing belongs to man, and man is nothing in comparison with God (55, 2).* This absoluteness of Allah is revolutionary, for it levels all mankind before his power. Allah is in total control of all things, and he has predetermined all life to follow in a certain pattern. There is perhaps no religious book that so stresses mankind's weakness in the face of God.

There is no priesthood in Islam such as developed in Christianity and other religions. All believers are held to be equally near to Allah, and Allah holds no special relationship with any man. Mohammad himself denied any supernatural or unique relationship with God, claiming only that he was a man like any other. Likewise, the wealthy and powerful of the world were warned that they owed their favored position not to their own worth, but to Allah's benevolence. "Whoso desireth power should know that all power belongeth to Allah" (35, 10). God will judge the powerful severely, the Koran says, if they oppress mankind. Leaders must consult with those they rule and know their desires. On the other hand, the wealthy, to earn Allah's favor, must "believe and do good" (34, 37). Greed and hoarding are roundly condemned, and money is to be used for the good of all. Usury, a common practice in Mohammad's time, is explicitly outlawed, and the wealthy are repeatedly reminded that one of their five chief responsibilities as believers is the support of the poor and needy. All men fall equally under the judgment of God.

It is wrong, however, to assume that this radical equalitarianism that levels all before Allah sanctions individualism and gives significance to each individual person. Islam did not develop the idea of the

* Numbers refer to standard chapter and verse in the Koran; see "Suggested Reading."

sanctity of each human being that became part of the European and American heritage. Islam emphasized rather the importance of the whole body of believers and stressed that each individual's importance lay in the role he played as one member of this body. The Muslim's duty was not self-assertion but submission to the will of God within the Islamic community.

This characteristic of submission was closely linked to another feature of the religion developed in the Koran. This feature was its fatalism or its tendency to ascribe all power and responsibility to Allah. At times this fatalism is so extreme that little is left to man but to obey and live out the predetermined course of events. "No soul can ever die except by Allah's leave and at the term appointed" (3, 145), the Holy Book warns at one point, and it consistently makes man a pawn or puppet of fate. The negative social and political aspects of such a belief will be seen in later Arab history.

The society envisioned by the Koran, therefore, was a community of believers living out their lives according to the strict code given Mohammad by Allah. Simplicity of life and moderation of habits were the great virtues, and one's eyes were to be set ultimately on heaven, which would be the reward given the man who followed Mohammad's teachings. Self-interest and personal advancement were to be submerged under the will of the whole body of believers, and all disputes or misunderstandings among the faithful were to be settled peacefully and rationally. Perhaps the greatest danger to the new faith lay in its own completeness. Because it boasted of offering an answer to every problem that might arise, it allowed no room for change or expansion. Mohammad had offered a solution to the crisis facing the Arab society of his day, but he could not anticipate what crises the Arab World might face in the future.

Mohammad had united the Arabian Peninsula by the time of his death and had so inspired his followers that they continued to conquer new territory and spread the new religion. Arab armies overran Iraq, Syria, Egypt, and all of North Africa. Spain and Persia were added as the Muslim armies marched farther east and west. Before the close of the eighth century, Islam had become a world religion and the Arabs rulers of an empire. For the next two centuries, the Middle East experienced a creative vigor and a vital, dynamic culture that it has not enjoyed since. Arab language and thought spread far and wide; poetry and art reached a perfection many modern scholars have admired. At a time when Europe was backward and impoverished, the Arab World was powerful, active, and wealthy.

The ideals that Mohammad had set forth through his personality and in the Koran, however, soon disappeared in practice as Arabs attempted to rule their far-flung empire. Leaders could not consult the governed, as the Koran commanded, when the governed were millions of people spread over thousands of miles speaking a variety of languages. In fact, the unity, stability, and order that Mohammad had given the Arabs had been challenged very soon after his death. Of the first five caliphs, or leaders of the faithful, who were elected to succeed the Prophet, four were assassinated or died under mysterious circumstances, victims of opponents who wanted the role of leader to fall to someone else. The command to settle disputes among themselves was forgotten, as Muslims divided into various groups, each supporting a different candidate for caliph, and each willing to go to war to ensure the succession of its candidate.

After the fifth caliph, the leadership came to reside in one family, for it was argued that the constant upheaval that followed the death of a caliph had to be brought to an end. The myth of election was maintained, however, and it was said that the caliphate was not hereditary, but passed from father to some other member of the family who was worthy to lead the faithful. Even this did not end the bickering, for as a result of the Muslim practice of taking more than one wife, there were always a number of sons and uncles interested in assuming power. Each of these possible heirs would gain followers and try to win control of the army, for success often meant how many soldiers could be mustered when the time to assume leadership came. Political upheaval thus became an institutionalized and anticipated part of Middle Eastern life. There seemed to be no way to assure peaceful succession of rulers, as developed elsewhere through hereditary monarchy, and the death of a caliph would be followed by a period of civil war. Indeed, the combatants struggled violently, for they knew that failure would mean death. The first act of a new caliph was to eliminate his opposition by murdering them. These changes of power, however, were rebellions and not revolutions—only those struggling for power were affected, while the vast majority of Arabs lived much the same as before, regardless of which leader or faction was in power.

In this sort of atmosphere it is not surprising that the caliphs amassed a great deal of power and wealth, seeking to maintain the armies that were the backbone of their security and status. The caliphs of the empire period of Arab history lost all contact with the simplicity and directness that had characterized the courts of Mohammad and the early caliphs. The capital was moved from the Arabian Peninsula, the birthplace of Islam, to Damascus, and later to wealthy and worldly Baghdad. The caliph assumed the splendor of Eastern rulers and demanded that his subjects prostrate themselves before him when they came into his presence.

The average Muslim came to see political life as far beyond his own power to influence or control. A political quietism and conservatism developed that argued that the good believer was to accept whatever government that existed, for that government had been instituted by Allah, and to challenge it was to challenge God himself. The intellectuals and religious leaders reinforced this quietism, by giving each succeeding government, no matter how violent its coming to power or how tenuous its claim to authority, the same approval and sanction. The saints and pious men of Islam refused to involve themselves with politics and argued that to do so was to compromise their faith and piety. They had forgotten Mohammad's own deep involvement in government and his hard work as leader of the faithful. Even the new sects that arose within Islam in opposition to orthodoxy and the prevailing authority reinforced this quietism and acceptance of the powers that be. As the dynamic and creative period of the Arab Empire came to an end, quietism became the chief characteristic of Arab society and remained, to this century, one of the greatest barriers to change and progress in the Middle East.

This submission to authority overtook other realms of Arab culture also. During the height of the empire, Muslim law—the Koran and the traditions concerning the sayings of the Prophet—were codified into a system that was to answer all legal problems that might arise. The learned men who prepared this code argued that it was complete and that no future judge would have to add to it or alter it, for it formed the guide given to mankind by Allah.

Art and poetry likewise underwent formalization. Rigid rules developed that governed the kind of work an artist or poet could produce. Innovation or change was considered dangerous to true piety and faith. Indeed, innovation in any aspect of life became one of the great sins of Islam, for it meant that the innovator found something wrong or amiss with the religious inheritance and that he wanted to alter the system established by Allah. Arab schools did not prize individuality among their pupils but trained them to memorize word for word the Koran and the other religious works. It was considered that all that was worth learning was contained in these books. Obedience was valued above all else in the students, and they were reminded that they formed part of the whole body of believers, whose duty it was to submit to God's will.

The submission to authority, the emphasis on obedience, and the rigid laws concerning every aspect of life created a split in Arab society between the governed and those who govern that grew wider as time passed. Government was remote from the masses of people, and they learned to expect nothing from those who ran their governments. No civic responsibility, no feeling that government had to take into consideration the needs and wants of the majority ever developed. The chief desire of the vast number of Arabs was to avoid government and to remove oneself as far as possible from its ravages, its ability to tax, seize property, and demand that a man serve in the army. No tradition was more detrimental to the development of Arab society than this lack of trust in government, and a problem of modern Arab leaders has been the building of respect for those who run the country. Centuries of government irresponsibility and violation of human rights must be repaired by the establishment of a true link between the rulers and the ruled. The ruled must be convinced that government can work for the benefit of all.

The two centuries of Arab greatness and vitality had seen the expansion of Islam over much of the earth and the establishment of an impressive empire. But as the original vigor of Arab civilization declined, only its weaknesses seemed to endure. Instead of a community of believers, there was civil strife and constant dispute. Instead of equality, there was tyranny and a class structure that guaranteed wealth and power to the very few and poverty to the majority. Instead of living lives in imitation of the Prophet, most Muslims remained worldly and guided by self-interest. As deterioration and change came to the Middle East, Islam offered no new guidelines to meet the new crisis. The faith became rigidified into old patterns and ideas, fearful of transformation and innovation. Had Mohammad appeared anew to guide believers into a new understanding of life, he would have been denounced as a heretic and driven from the presence of the faithful.

After 950 the Arab Empire dissolved rapidly, and in its place a new people eventually established power and domination. The Turks, originally from Central Asia, had been invited to the Middle East by the caliphs who wanted them to serve as palace guards and soldiers. But by the middle of the thirteenth century they were firmly in control. They moved the center of their empire away from the Arab World, ultimately choosing Istanbul, the former Byzantine city of Constantinople, to be their capital. The Turkish sultan took on the duties and functions of the caliph, and the Arabs became second-class citizens in a Turkish Empire. The Arabs fell into the political and economic backwardness from which they have only recently begun to recover.

The Ottoman Empire exacerbated the worst aspects and traditions of the Arab Empire. The problem of succession, never solved by the caliphs, became the paramount concern of the sultans. Possible rivals to the throne were kept in cages from the time of birth so that they would never be physically or emotionally capable of governing. Sometimes sultans resorted to wholesale slaughter of all possible contenders, and since any male member of the family could be elected, this meant that uncles, cousins, nephews, brothers, and sons had to be eliminated. Mehmed III (1595–1603) executed nineteen brothers and two of his own sons to secure his eight years of reign.

Political upheaval, civil war, and coup d'état likewise remained a part of Middle Eastern life. Each possible heir to the sultan's chair gained followers and tried to acquire the support of the army or important military leaders. The political system remained intimately tied to military power and strength. Even regions such as Algeria, that never fell totally under Turkish sway but paid tribute to the sultan, were plagued by political disorder. In Algeria, fourteen of the thirty rulers between 1671 and 1818 rose to power by murdering their predecessors. In such societies, little value is placed on legitimacy and order, on civic responsibility, or on the peaceful settlement of disputes. All value resides in force and strength. The present-day military rulers in the Middle East and North Africa are part of a long tradition that grants precedence to the man with a weapon.

Since values were primarily military, the tilling of the soil or the raising of livestock provided little respect or honor for the peasant. Often the peasant lost all of his land and livelihood because of the heavy duties and taxes that the government and the men in power placed on him. The result was the creation of a growing class of dispossessed and discontented people, who turned to rebellion, banditry, and other forms of violence to express their dissatisfaction with society. Turkish society was strongly hierarchical, with full social and economic benefits going only to those at the top. The vast majority of people, the peasantry and the poor of the cities, faced economic oppression and social discrimination.

At the height of their empire, the Turks presented a threat to Europe and had stretched their power throughout the Middle East into the Balkans, twice besieging Vienna. But by the nineteenth century, the Ottoman Empire was going the way of the Arab Empire centuries earlier. The power of the sultan declined, and many areas of his once vast domains began to slip away. His empire was known as the "sick man of Europe"; many expansionists and colonialists in Europe looked forward to the day when Turkish territory could be divided among Britain, France, and the other powers.

Indeed, the European nations were not long in taking advantage of the power vacuum in the Middle East to assert their claims. France seized Algeria in 1830. Britain occupied Egypt in 1882, claiming that her presence would be a short one. She remained until 1956. When the Ottoman Empire finally disappeared from history at the end of World War I, England took Iraq, and France, Syria. Indeed, by 1920, the vast majority of the Arab World was ruled by Europe, and only Saudi Arabia and Yemen could claim any degree of independence.

The disappearance of the Turk and the appearance of the European began the introduction of the Middle East to the modern world. Arabs were made aware of modern technology and of modern ideas concerning government and society. Since the Europeans were interested in profiting from the agricultural and mineral wealth of their colonies, they brought with them modern agricultural techniques and built irrigation systems to water arid land. Commerce and trade were expanded, railways built, the highway and water systems renovated and extended. Some effort was even made to improve the quality of life for the average Arab—headway was made against the plague, and a few schools and colleges were established, most often by Christian missionaries hoping to convert the Muslims.

But the overall effect of colonialism was as stifling and regressive as the years of Turkish domination had been. Europeans boasted of teaching the Arabs good government and enlightened leadership but did little to give the Arabs a sense of self-esteem or a belief in their own ability. European racist attitudes were obvious. The English in Egypt did not mingle with the Egyptians, but ruled them from a distance through puppet monarchs who would not go against British interests. In Algeria, where hundreds of thousands of French settlers came (Algeria is only a few hundred miles from Marseille) to create a greater France, the Arabs were second-class citizens, enjoying none of the rights of the French settlers. There is no better example of the European attitude toward the Arab than the fact that the French governor of Algeria in the middle of the nineteenth century rode to the theater on the backs of his Arab servants.

In Algeria the French destroyed the old tribal leaders and discredited the old religious and social elite. In Egypt, Syria, and Iraq, however, the Europeans attempted to rule with the tribal chieftains, wealthy merchants, and others who were willing to cooperate. These chieftains and merchants were often the most conservative members of Arab society, opposing all change or improvement. Often too these men were unscrupulous and cooperated with the colonial powers only for their own monetary gain. Thus European rule, though it brought modern technology and new ideas to the Arab World, likewise reinforced old patterns of political life that had for centuries kept the Middle East stagnating and backward.

In the last thirty years of European rule, the standard of living in Egypt actually declined. In the same period, Syria and Iraq were torn between conservative factions maintained in power by Western interests and nationalist factions fighting for independence and reform. In Algeria, after some hope that the Arabs might gain equality with the French, it became obvious that the French had no serious desire to relinquish their social and economic privileges. In each of the Arab nations where radical governments later appeared, the crisis between the old order and the new generation's demands for change took on enormous proportions, creating tension that often broke out into violence and bloodshed. Many articulate Arabs were humiliated by the social and economic poverty of their world; they deeply resented European superiority and strength and felt that they could no longer endure the treatment they received as inferiors and underlings.

The crisis that affected the Arab World in the twentieth century was therefore a crisis that encompassed all aspects of society. The political system had been corrupted by centuries of tyranny under despotic Arab and Turkish rulers. The man who came to power was not always the ablest and wisest man available, but far more often was the man with the strongest military force backing him. Those in power did little or nothing to aid the less fortunate; most people feared government and wanted to keep themselves as far as possible from its ravages. The centuries of misrule had accentuated the fatalism and quietism that was so much a part of Islamic belief, causing Arabs to assume that nothing could be done to alleviate their condition. Society and economy had stagnated and fallen far behind the more advanced areas of the world; the vast majority of people were plagued by a system that looked to the past for answers that were not forthcoming. Arab civilization had grown rigid and unchangeable; for centuries, new ideas and attitudes had been weeded out by Islamic wisemen who denounced any change from age-old religious law. The vicious circle of poverty, ignorance, and backwardness seemed unbreakable: how could a people convinced that they were living as Allah intended them to live acquire the optimism and hope that are necessary for progress? how could a poor and illiterate people obtain the wealth and knowledge that their very poverty and ignorance forced them to be without?

Yet the Middle East was not without hope, for during the time that the Europeans occupied the Arab World, and began to make their interests and power felt, there began the long process of Arab awakening that was to result in the breaking of the vicious circle. Slowly, new attitudes toward life began to develop among a few Arabs who became convinced that meaningful change was possible. The discovery of new values and the development of a faith in progress and in the human ability to transform the world spread among a few enlightened souls. Nowhere is this process better represented than in the autobiography of Taha Husain, the great Egyptian writer and educator. Husain tells of how, as a student, he suddenly comprehended that his own blindness and the death of his four-year-old sister were not part of Allah's will or the overall scheme of things, but were rather the results of his people's ignorance and indifference to human suffering. He realized that his blindness and his sister's death might have been avoided if change were permitted to work its way into Middle Eastern life. In his new vision, he saw that his people could improve themselves only by a radical transformation of attitude and belief. Self-help and progress were possible, but they required the hard work of abandoning the values held sacred for centuries. The past, however dear, had to be forgotten. When Taha Husain published his autobiography in 1926, only a minority of Arabs had come to see the truth of his vision. Even now, the long process of intellectual and moral awakening is far from complete, but the Arab World has come a long way, and it is safe to say that the ignorance that caused Husain's blindness and the death of his young sister has largely disappeared. New attitudes and ways of doing things have come to the Middle East. After this survey of the factors that brought about Arab decline and stagnation, it is only fair to turn now to the elements that have contributed to revival and improvement.

CHAPTER THREE

The Arab National Awakening

A genuine change in society does not take place overnight. Several generations are needed to transform attitudes and customs held sacred for centuries and to convince men that there are new and better ways of doing things. The traditional manner of life has to be discredited; there must be an active search for social and political philosophies that might solve the problems that plague the old order. The great revolutions of the modern world—the American, the French, the Russian, and the Chinese—were each preceded by long periods of discussion and soul-searching. It took men many years to comprehend their predicament and to decide that action was required. It is not surprising, then, that the Arab Awakening has been a long, slow process that is yet far from completion. Arabs have had to look into their past and discard what they found detrimental or worthless. They have had to experiment with new ideas and concepts and find some system that fits their peculiar needs and traditions. They have had to do all this in the presence of an appalling poverty and ignorance that has held progress back at every point. Few peoples have had to work against such odds.

The awakening began about a hundred and fifty years ago in what is today Syria and Lebanon among a few scholars and poets who were concerned about the backwardness of their language and culture. Arabic had always been sacred to the Arabs—it was the language of the Koran and other religious works and was studied as a means of understanding God and his wishes for mankind. But in the centuries of Arab decline, the language had become corrupted and had fallen into disuse. It had let the modern world pass it by. There were no words to describe the achievements of modern science and engineering; there was no vocabulary that could be employed to discuss new social and economic ideas. If an Arab wanted to learn about these things, he had to study a foreign language—English or French —and travel to Europe where there were books and universities. Libraries and schools that offered a wide range of knowledge were nonexistent in the Middle East.

American Protestant missionaries aided the Arabs who wanted to revive and modernize their language. The Americans brought printing presses and money to pay for the production of books and journals. Indeed, several Americans devoted themselves wholeheartedly to the project. They established schools to educate young Arabs and a college, the American University of Beirut, that trained teachers for the new schools. Ibrahim, who ruled Syria from 1832 to 1840, supported their work and was himself a forward-looking leader who hoped to instill in his people a love for the Arab past. Mohammad Ali, Ibrahim's father and the governor of Egypt, likewise knew the value of education, and took similar measures. He sent promising young Egyptians to France and England to study modern science and engineering; he brought books and teachers from Europe to Cairo to train young officers in the Egyptian military schools. Because of these early efforts, Syria and Egypt became the centers of the Arab revival, attracting young Arabs from many parts of the Middle East.

For the first time books and newspapers began to appear on a regular basis in Arabic. By 1870 an Arabic dictionary had appeared and an encyclopedia soon followed. Learned Arabs began to form literary societies that discussed a wide range of topics from Arab history to the effect of Western ideas on traditional Arab life. It was in these small and harmless societies that the first germ of revival was spread. Young poets wrote works that longed for the return of the Arab World to greatness. These poems were circulated clandestinely from group to group and read in secret so that the Turkish authorities would not put an end to the societies.

The revival of language and literature brought about a revival of interest in all aspects of life. Talented men began to examine their world and to wonder why decline had come. Others concerned themselves with plans for the future and looked to the period of Arab greatness for the strengths they felt might once again cause the Arab World to become vigorous and creative. It was inevitable that these men would turn first to religion, for it had been Islam that had molded the Arab people into a civilization. As language and literature revived, men's minds turned to the Koran and to Mohammad to learn again the tradition that had grown so stale and shopworn after centuries of repetition and stagnation.

One of the first wise men to examine the faith and discover what words it held for the modern world and for the Arab future was the wandering preacher Jamal al-Din al-Afghani. Al-Afghani was born in Persia in 1838 but traveled widely through the Middle East and Europe. He lived for a long time in Egypt, where he gained a large number of followers and exerted a long-lasting influence. For al-Afghani, the Islamic teaching most important for the modern world was unity. Arabs had allowed themselves to fall apart and to quarrel with one another. Rulers had followed their own selfish ambitions; the common man had forgotten his duty as a member of the community of the faithful. Muslims needed to return to Mohammad's conception of a unified, peaceful society that found its true meaning in submission to God and to the rules of the Koran.

But there was likewise a great deal that was modern in al-Afghani's teaching. He told his followers that they should turn their eyes toward this world and make it a good place to live in. Allah had not meant that men should resign themselves to intolerable conditions; indeed, the Prophet himself had not accepted the world as he had found it but had worked to change and improve it. Al-Afghani wanted to wipe out the fatalism and the quiet acceptance of circumstance that had become so much a part of the Arab character. He wanted to convince his people that meaningful reform was possible, that man could alter this world by working on it. He pointed to the achievements of modern science and technology as proof of man's ability and intelligence. These discoveries and inventions, he said, were not for Europeans alone but for the whole world, and the Arabs should have their fair share.

But al-Afghani did not stop at advocating material improvement. He went on to urge political activity and even to call for the assassination of Arab leaders who did not rule justly or who stood in the way of Arab progress and revival. Some of his young disciples were to put this teaching into effect. Al-Afghani's hopes for the Middle East were for a revived people, unified and given direction by their faith, but with new confidence and pride in what they could achieve this side of the grave.

His disciple Mohammad Abduh (1849–1905) was even more on the side of modernization. After a radical youth, in which he had been forced into exile for his extreme opinions, Mohammad Abduh returned to Egypt to become the highest ranking Arab in the British administration of the colony. He used his powerful position to spread his ideas of reform and change. Al-Azhar, the thousand-year-old center of Muslim theology and learning, was modernized and the student body enlarged. New faculties of medicine, science, and engineering were created. Mohammad Abduh argued that he loved Islam as much as the most devout conservative but feared what might happen to the Arab World if some accommodation to change and progress were not made. He wanted to preserve the good things of the faith—its deep concern for community, its profound faith in God—but discard those things that had become detrimental to society, such as the fear of modern learning and the inferior status of women. Where religious tradition conflicted with the best of new ideas, religion had to change and make way for the modern world.

Not all religious thinkers, however, were aligned with al-Afghani and Mohammad Abduh. Some felt that these two men were too willing to adopt European ideas and customs and that they did not see that the Arab World could be destroyed if it borrowed European ways without close and careful consideration. The Arabs could find their own path to modernity and did not have to follow a path offered by foreigners. Chief among these more conservative thinkers was Rashid Rida (1865–1935), who had gone to Cairo in the 1890s to work with Mohammad Abduh but had quickly abandoned the master's ideas for his own conception of the Arab future.

Rida was not an unthinking conservative who accepted the whole past as good and necessary. Indeed, he had little use for the religious leaders who reacted blindly to the crisis the Arab World was facing and felt that things could go on as they always had. For Rida, what was required was a return to the values expressed in the Koran and in the words of the Prophet. He wanted to erase a thousand years of history that he felt had been corrupted by Turkish and foreign rule. If the Arabs were to revive, they had to return to the principles of pure Arabism that were expressed in the earliest days of Arab greatness. Arab civilization had a greatness and a subtlety that few foreigners could comprehend, and this greatness and subtlety should not be allowed to disappear. The adoption of modern European ideas would be as great a disaster for the Arab people as the submission to Turkish rule had been. Arabs would lose contact with their past and become a rootless people. For Rida, then, the Koran and true religious faith offered no conflict with the modern world; what conflicted with the modern world were the centuries of misrule and stagnation when the Arabs had not been allowed to express their true values.

The concern for the faith that al-Afghani, Mohammad Abduh, and Rashid Rida showed soon spread throughout the Arab World. Young men in Damascus, Cairo, Algiers, and elsewhere took new interest in their faith and found inspiration in its teachings. Inspired by Mohammad Abduh, and especially by Rashid Rida, Ben Badis of Algeria founded a movement that sought, as early as 1912, to loosen the hold French culture had on Algerian young men and women and to reinstill pride in Islam and Arab history. Ben Badis and his followers adopted the slogan "Islam is my religion; Arabic is my language; Algeria is my fatherland." For the first time, young Algerians were given an alternative to the culture forced on them by their colonial masters.

The religious revival never lost its hold on the Arab Awakening. It underlined the importance of religion in the life of every Arab, an importance that is still respected by Arab socialists. But most important, the concern for religion assured that the Arab Awakening would be a search for the true roots and values of Arab history. By focusing attention on the faith, al-Afghani, Mohammad Abduh, and Rashid Rida inspired later Arabs to reject any ideology that did not smack of Arab tradition; future Arab thinkers and activists would be careful to examine their thought and work in the light of history. In a very real sense, Arab radicals today see their achievements not as revolution and total change, but rather as a return to what is best in the past.

While these men concentrated on religion, other, more restless Arabs began to organize and take action against tyranny and foreign rule. They felt deeply incensed and humiliated by Arab weakness and lack of independence. A growing sense of national pride and self-esteem created in them a desire for freedom and the right to govern themselves. At first this nationalist spirit appeared rarely and gained only a few adherents; it took two generations for it to blossom into a movement of strength and vitality, followed by the majority of Arab people. But nationalism became the single most important force in the Arab Awakening, causing men who had remained indifferent to political life for centuries to demand change and transformation.

In the early 1870s, Mohammad al-Moquani of Algeria led his people in revolt against the French, a rebellion that was subdued only after much destruction and bloodshed. In the early '80s, anti-British sentiment arose in Egypt under the nationalist Colonel Ahmad Urabi, who had grown concerned over European control of Egyptian finances and economy. Peace was restored when the British army occupied the country. The British Prime Minister, William Gladstone, declared that his country would remain only a short time, but the British did not leave until 1956, when they were forced out by another nationalist colonel, Gamel Abdel Nasser. Urabi's movement had been supported by al-Afghani and his followers, who formed the National Party to fight for independence. Mohammad Abduh had been active in the cause and was forced into exile when the British seized the country.

After the revolts by al-Moquani and Urabi, nationalism was quiet in the Middle East for several decades, but it was a deceptive quiet. Small groups of men were meeting secretly in the larger Arab cities, planning for the day when Turkish and European rulers would be overthrown. By the turn of the century, the spirit of nationalism and reform had taken deeper root than was apparent to the casual observer. By the outbreak of World War I in 1914 nationalism had gained an impetus it was never to lose.

In the early years of this century, several Arabs who were officers in the Turkish army joined the Committee of Union and Progress, known to history as the Young Turks. The Young Turk organization had been founded by a group of liberals who were opposed to the rigid tyranny of Sultan Abdul Hamid, one of the most despotic rulers of modern history. The Arab officers had joined their fellow Turkish officers, for they felt a common purpose in bringing an end to Abdul

Hamid's rule. In 1908 the Young Turks were successful beyond their wildest dreams. The Sultan was forced to accept reforms, and a year later he was driven from the throne in favor of a more moderate ruler.

But the Arabs soon discovered that the Young Turks had no intention of granting freedom to the Arab World. The Young Turks continued to rule the Ottoman Empire from Constantinople and rigged elections so that Arabs were not fairly represented in the new parliament. The Arabs swallowed their sense of betrayal and organized new groups to press for freedom and self-government. They realized that they outnumbered the Turks within the empire and knew that they could make their influence felt eventually. Rashid Rida, who had supported the Young Turks, helped form a new party, the Decentralization Party, a group that demanded a status for Arabs equal to that enjoyed by the Turks. The Decentralization Party did not want to destroy the empire, but to divide it evenly between its Arab and Turkish populations. It was the first political movement to attempt to reach a large number of people, and it opened centers in villages and towns throughout the Middle East. For the first time the average Arab experienced political discussion and debate.

More radical activists, however, were forming groups more deeply opposed to Turkish rule. The most important of these was al-Fatat, or the Young Arab Society, founded in Paris in 1911 by seven Arab students. After two years it moved to Beirut and then to Damascus, where the membership grew to more than two hundred. It imposed a rigorous process of membership upon those who wished to join. Each individual was closely scrutinized to see if he could be trusted. Only the strongest and most committed were allowed to join. They had to pledge full obedience to the society and promise that they would die before they revealed the purpose and goals of the organization. The screening process worked, for no member betrayed the society, even though several were tortured and executed by Turkish authorities. The army likewise had its secret society, known as al-Ahd, or the Covenant. Both al-Ahd and al-Fatat were dedicated to complete independence; they were the most profound examples up to that time of the growing fervor of Arab nationalism.

World War I helped precipitate Arab activity and zeal. The Turks entered the war on the side of Germany and Austria-Hungary against the French and English. Young Arabs were faced with a dilemma: should they fight with the Turks who refused to grant them freedom, or should they join the French and British who fought against the Turks, but who were not Muslims. The issue was complicated by the Sultan, who declared the war to be Jihad, or Holy War, and ordered the faithful to join the Turkish ranks.

From their base in Egypt, the English carried on an active campaign to convert Arabs in Syria, Iraq, and the Arabian Peninsula to the side of France and England. Promises were made to Arab leaders granting independence to the Arab nations following the war and denying any British or French colonial interest in the Arab countries then under Turkish rule. By 1916 many Arabs were convinced that their future lay with the West; even al-Fatat cautiously agreed to support the British. Arab units were formed that sabotaged Turkish installations and railroads; Arabs fought alongside British soldiers to free Palestine and Syria from Turkish control. This was the time of the legendary Lawrence of Arabia, the extraordinary Englishman who led Arab warriors on surprise attacks against enemy forts and encampments.

But the Arabs were destined to be as disappointed in the British as they had been in the Young Turks. When the war came to an end, Britain occupied Iraq, Jordan, and Palestine, while France seized Syria, forcing the popular King Faisal into exile. Only Saudi Arabia and Yemen, among the Arab nations, could claim any degree of independence. A second disappointment came when the British Prime Minister, David Balfour, in what has come to be known as the Balfour Declaration, announced that Palestine would become a homeland for Jews who wished to settle there. Two heavy blows had been given to Arab nationalism: the Turks had been replaced by new masters, and Palestine, an area that had been Arab for thirteen hundred years, had been promised to a people the Arabs felt had no claim to it.

These setbacks, however, only helped to consolidate Arab determination to drive the foreigners from the Middle East and gain independence. The years after World War I were characterized by violence and disorder as the Arab Awakening took on a greater intensity and depth. Outwardly, the Arabs adopted the trappings of Western parliamentary government as it was practiced in England, France, and the United States. Inwardly, however, the Arab spirit was in great turmoil and showed increasing dissatisfaction with colonialism, occupation, and exploitation. For liberal democracy was not the only experiment; the Arabs also tried fascism, socialism, and other political ideologies in an attempt to find some answer to the crisis. The overriding concern became independence at any cost, and little thought was given to social or economic reform.

In Egypt, the prominent nationalist party after the war was the Wafd, or Delegation Party. The Wafd was named for the unsuccessful delegation of Egyptians that had gone to Versailles where the victorious powers were negotiating a peace treaty to plead the Egyptian cause and ask for independence. Britain, France, and the other nations at the peace conference refused to hear the party, and it returned to Cairo without one concession. Saad Zaghlul (1857?–1927), who had led the delegation, emerged as the most important political leader in Egypt. As a young man, Zaghlul, a follower of al-Afghani, had become convinced of the need for reform. He was an admirer of representative government and thought that Egypt should adopt such a system if it were given its freedom.

In the tense years following World War I, Zaghlul and his party guided Egypt into partial independence and agreement with Britain to allow limited self-determination. Between 1918 and 1922, the British had their hands full trying to maintain order and peace. Demonstrations, riots, and assassinations became commonplace. A commission sent by the British government to study the Egyptian question recommended that a constitution be granted and concessions be made to Egyptian popular opinion. This was done, and the Egyptians were permitted to elect a National Assembly. Zaghlul and the Wafd led the new government and continued to apply pressure, hoping to gain further concessions. But the British refused any further liberties; their army remained in Egypt to protect British lives and property and to guard the Suez Canal, England's gateway to India and the East.

The Wafd was the first great political party of Egyptian history and contributed greatly to Egypt's revival and awakening. It was well organized throughout the country, reaching students, urban workers, peasants, and many others. For the first time, many Egyptians were introduced to politics and given a sense of participation in national life. During the '20s and '30s, the Wafd functioned as the chief expression of nationalist sentiment, balancing the interests of the Egyptian people against those of the king and the British. But it failed to solve the general political and social crisis the country faced. It based its hopes on eventual British withdrawal and on representative government, both of which failed to materialize or work. The British stayed on, their presence a continual reminder of Egypt's lack of freedom. The National Assembly disintegrated into a center of bickering and quarreling. The Wafd itself became corrupt; political offices were bought and sold and party leaders became defenders of the status quo, refusing to consider change or reform. It was impossible that European-style democracy would function in a country that had no democratic liberal traditions and where the vast majority of people were illiterate.

In Syria the nationalists were able to gain less than they had in Egypt. Anti-French sentiment was strong and widespread, but unfocused and without direction. In 1925 a full-scale rebellion broke out among the Druze, a Muslim sect that had preserved its own traditions for centuries. They resented French encroachment on what they considered to be their inherited rights. The rebellion soon spread to the whole country and lasted two years. The French restored order at the cost of many lives on both sides, but agreed to grant a constitution and permit elections on the basis of universal manhood suffrage. Syrian nationalists formed a Popular Front Party that hoped to gain further freedom. Representative government failed in Syria, however, as it had in Egypt, and for the same reasons. The Popular Front was incapable of driving the French out, and the National Assembly was impotent and chaotic. Men who have had no political experience cannot, overnight, adopt a system of government that took centuries to evolve in the West.

In Iraq too the colonial period was marked by violence and frustration. From the beginning, Iraqis fought the British and demanded their independence. Peace was restored when the British invited King Faisal, the popular Arab leader who had been driven from Syria, to become the ruler. Faisal governed well until his death in 1933, balancing the various ethnic and religious groups of Iraq, and bringing a stability that Iraq has not enjoyed since. But the unity he maintained collapsed upon his death, and no leader emerged of comparable ability. By the end of the '30s, Iraq was governed by a strong man, Nuri al-Said, who created a police state and eliminated those who dared oppose him. Nuri al-Said was committed to the status quo and to the British presence. He feared the growth of Arab nationalism, for Iraq had many non-Arab people who would have nothing to do with it. He feared reform or change of any kind that might pull him from power, and he looked to the British to support him and maintain him in power. Government in Iraq became a nightmare that would take years to reform or improve; here, the Arab Awakening had its most severe challenge to make right the misrule and tyranny created during the colonial period.

Only in Algeria were the two decades following World War I peaceful and orderly. Algerian leaders hoped for moderate reform and envisioned no separation from the mother country. Indeed, most Algerians seemed satisfied with their connection to France and felt that national improvement could come through alliance with the French authorities. Ferhat Abbas, one of the first great leaders of modern Algeria, wrote that no Algerian nation had ever existed, and that Algerian nationalism was an impossibility. All was not completely well, however, for many Arab Algerians had grown weary at the superior status granted the French who lived in North Africa. They wanted the right to vote, hold office, and the other privileges granted the lowest Frenchman. They looked to France to grant these rights and to establish genuine democracy in Algeria. World War II helped to precipitate these demands. Algerians fought and died alongside Europeans to free France from the Nazi occupation. When the French granted only token change, many Algerians grew angered; some joined the radical nationalist party, the North African Star, founded in 1926 by Messali Hadj, which had remained small and insignificant until French intransigence drove many moderates into the extremist camp. By 1945, violence had come to Algeria as it had two decades earlier to Egypt, Syria, and Iraq. Many were convinced that only force would cause the French to grant independence. Liberal democracy—the government dear to the hearts of many Frenchmen—was discredited in the minds of Algerians because liberal and democratic Frenchmen had refused to guarantee even the most basic rights to Arabs.

As Western representative government proved unworkable in Egypt, Syria, Iraq, and Algeria, other ideologies appeared and held men's allegiance for a while. The largest and most dramatic of these alternative philosophies was the Muslim Brotherhood, or *Ikhwan*, a reactionary and totalitarian organization that was founded in 1929 in Egypt by Hassan al-Banna. Al-Banna fiercely rejected all that was new and modern. He demanded total adherence to Muslim Law and urged his followers to punish or execute any Muslim who failed to live according to the religious code. Al-Banna rejected Rashid Rida as too moderate; true religion demanded passionate commitment and action. With all the devotion of the true believer and fanatic, al-Banna felt justified in using any means to destroy those who refused his message.

The Brotherhood developed a whole social and political system based on the Koran. The poor and needy were to be cared for by a revival of the commandment to show compassion for and support the less fortunate. Law was to be changed to correspond exactly with the Holy Book. Leaders were to be accountable to the law, and a strict code of business and political ethics was established so that corruption in government and elsewhere would disappear. The Brotherhood demanded high standards for all Arabs and preached the responsibility of all in the improvement of society. It is easy to understand the appeal the Brotherhood had to idealistic Arabs caught up in the tensions created by modernization. It offered simple solutions to complex problems and offered a whole way of life to men whose world seemed to be slipping from them, for the Brotherhood demanded blind and unquestioning obedience from each of its members. None were to flinch from death and none were to refuse to carry out the commands of superiors in the organization. An underground military force was created to sabotage the Wafd and other political parties with which the Brotherhood disagreed. Muslim brothers learned how to use rifles, grenades, and machine guns. They were trained in terrorist and guerrilla activity, and they carried out many of the assassinations and violent demonstrations that racked the Middle East in the 1940s. From Egypt, the Brotherhood spread to other Arab countries, particularly Syria and Iraq. By 1950 it was said to have at least fifteen hundred active organizations working throughout the Arab World.

Fascism too gained a following in the years of tension and stress that preceded World War II. In Egypt, Ahmed Hussein founded his

Young Egypt, an organization modeled on the Hitler Youth. He dreamed of an Egyptian Empire that would join Nazi Germany and Fascist Italy in the struggle against the corrupt Western democracies. Indeed, many Egyptians were impressed by the efforts of Hitler and Mussolini to unify and strengthen their countries. If fascism worked so successfully in Europe, wouldn't it likewise prove beneficial in the Middle East? Anwar Sadat, now the President of Egypt, was attracted to fascism for a while as a young man, for he saw in it the means to force the English out and bring Egypt around to greatness. In Syria, fascism took the form of the Syrian National Party, a group which claimed that Syrians were racially and historically the supreme people of the Middle East. A Syrian Empire, stretching from the Mediterranean Sea to the Persian Gulf, was claimed as the natural right of the Syrian nation. In Iraq, fascists nearly seized power at the beginning of World War II, but were successfully overcome by the dictator, Nuri al-Said, with the aid of the British.

If the Muslim Brotherhood and fascism appealed to the extreme right, socialism was adopted by the extreme left. Communist parties first appeared in Egypt in the years after World War I. By the early '30s cells were active in Syria and Iraq, and there were a few communists in Algeria. But these early groups were small and ineffectual. Often they were made up of Jewish, Armenian, or other non-Arab intellectuals who had little feeling for the needs of the average Arab. Their socialism tended to be doctrinaire, and it rejected Arab nationalism as a reactionary and nonrevolutionary movement.

But as discontent and dissatisfaction with colonialism grew in the '30s and '40s, the number of Arab communists likewise grew. Communism offered a whole social and economic system that claimed to answer the needs of nations long exploited and misused; it had been successful in turning Russia into a first-rate power in a few short decades. Also, it was the sworn enemy of the West and condemned the European powers with the same vehemence used by Arab nationalists. Communist groups have never been large in the Middle East—only two thousand party members existed in Egypt at the time of the party's greatest strength—but they have exerted an influence greater than their small membership would indicate. In Syria, under the leadership of Khalid Bakdash, they have been most successful of all. In organizing the Syrian party, Bakdash was careful to emphasize the similarities between communism and the Islamic idea of community. He argued that Islam was genuinely communistic and that the believer could easily adopt Marxism without compromising his faith or his adherence to the law. Because of Bakdash's careful work, communism took deeper root in Syria than elsewhere in the Arab World, and to this day plays a significant part in Syrian national life.

In this survey of Arab political life following World War I, two features stand out: the phenomenal growth of nationalism and the desire for independence, and the failure of the Arabs to find a political and social philosophy to match their desire for independence. In each Arab country under discussion, nationalism had reached a fever pitch by 1945. Violence had become a daily occurrence, and no government could maintain order and stability. At the same time, no ideology had emerged that gave coherence and meaning to the Arab Awakening. Parliamentary government had failed miserably, for it had been a halfhearted and superficial attempt to graft Western ways upon a part of the world that had very different traditions and background. The Muslim Brotherhood appealed only to the more violent and rootless elements of society. Fascism lost its attraction with the defeat of Hitler and Mussolini. Communism drew only a small number of followers and remained incomprehensible to the majority. Without ideology and direction, the Arab Awakening remained incomplete and the Arab World resembled a man driven by one overwhelming desire—to obtain his freedom and independence—but with no plan of how to obtain his desire.

By 1940, however, a new group of thinkers emerged who looked carefully at Arab nationalism and developed systems of thought based on what they considered to be the deepest and most important elements of Arab history. Working in the same tradition as the earlier religious thinkers—al-Afghani, Mohammad Abduh, and Rashid Rida —this new group knew that it was important to isolate and preserve those things that were uniquely Arab. They recognized that parliamentary democracy and the other ideologies had failed because they had failed to touch the mainstream of Arab life. This new generation of writers, therefore, borrowed ideas from the West, from socialism, fascism, from the Muslim Brotherhood, and from many other sources, blending them into systems that spoke eloquently to Arab needs and hopes. With them, the Arab Awakening reached a new level of understanding and comprehension; the whole crisis that had come to the Middle East was seen and remedies were offered that covered the whole gamut of experience.

One such writer of importance was Abdullah al-Alayili, who published the *National Constitution of the Arabs* in 1941. In his book al-Alayili looked at the idea of nationalism. True nationalism, he said, was far more complex than an ardent desire for independence. True nationalism consisted of five elements, each of which must be explored and developed by a people if a genuine and strong nation were to be created. First, language was "the essential pillar" upon which everything else was based. Second, environment was important, for a nation needed an environment common to all its people to give them similar backgrounds and interests. Third, ancestry was important, for common ties of blood and race gave a nation an even stronger feeling of destiny and shared goals. Next, history was important because the people of a nation needed fixed points in the past that all could look to for guidance and inspiration. Finally, shared customs were the last ingredient of nationalism. The Arab people shared all five points in abundance, al-Alayili wrote, and careful nursing of each would produce the sort of society that was needed. The supreme duty of every Arab was to make these elements an essential part of his character and personality. For every Arab, nationalism should become a sacred religion, a "compulsive instinct."

But al-Alayili's most interesting idea was his belief that the Arab people needed a leader—"powerful and violent"—to mold them together. This leader had to be ascetic and lead a pure, clean life. He must be in contact with the deepest spiritual aspirations of his people and have their respect and esteem. And this leader must rule despotically, for only by so doing could he create the unity and common purpose essential to Arab development. Al-Alayili drew his vision of a powerful leader in part from history, from the stories surrounding Mohammad and the early caliphs, inspired, charismatic leaders who had molded the faithful together.

Al-Alayili's thought was complex and was read primarily by intellectuals, but a second writer of this new group of thinkers, Sati al-Husri, was more widely read and influential among a larger number of people. Al-Husri's essential point was that two elements give a people distinction and make of them a nation. These were history and language, for by them a man is defined and he is able to express what is of value to him. Al-Husri concluded, therefore, that there is no true freedom for an individual outside of his nation, outside of his language and history. These he must cultivate. Indeed, the only freedom available to man is obtained by losing oneself in one's nation. Here al-Husri used the same word for "lose" that the Muslim mystics had used when they described the mystical experience of losing oneself in God, and al-Husri seems to have meant the word in the same sense the mystics had: the individual must desire to make himself part of the whole, for without this, he is nothing. Al-Husri went further than the traditional idea of community in Islam, where the common man and the leader were bound by a contract under God established by religious law. For al-Husri, nothing short of complete obedience on the part of the common man to the will of the state was demanded, regardless of religious law and the tenets of Islam.

But the most significant thinker to develop his thought in this period was Michael Aflaq. Aflaq was born in Syria of Christian parents, but he has always considered himself first of all an Arab. He developed early an interest in Arabic language and literature, and it was while he was a student of literature at the Sorbonne that he and a fellow student, Salah Bitar, who was a law student, founded the Baath Party. Baath means resurrection in Arabic, and Aflaq and Bitar intended nothing less than the resurrection of Arab society. Aflaq took ideas from the great French writers André Gide and Romain Rolland, whom he called "noble souls," and from German writers such as Herder and Hegel, from whom he learned to look for the deeper meaning in history, beyond mere external events and economic factors, and molded them into a system of his own.

Aflaq begins with history and religion. He turns back to the early period of Islam and to Mohammad, and says that the Koran and the Prophet together represent the deepest tendencies of the Arab World. Not only did the Arab World truly begin with them; they likewise indicate the ideas and goals toward which the Arabs inevitably tend. Islam and Arabism are the same; it is the duty of every Arab youth to imitate Mohammad.

The essense of Islam, Aflaq goes on, is humanism, a mode of

conduct and life that is deeply civilized and admirable. Just as it was the duty of the early conquests of Islam to bring this message to the world, to conquer in order to civilize according to Islamic teachings, so it is the duty of the present generation to return to Islamic humanism and again set an example for the world to see and admire. Aflaq argues that Arab humanism cannot be reestablished unless there is a total, violent revolution that wrenches the Arabs from their immediate past and sets them on a new course. A total change is needed in the psychological make-up of the average Arab; he must devote himself entirely to revolution and change. The Arabs must develop a powerful hatred, a hatred unto death for all those who do not embody the nationalist ideal or who do not involve themselves in the struggle. Violence must be done, for only violence cleanses and makes new.

It is the young who must make the revolution, Aflaq continues, for only the young are free of the cynicism and pessimism that come with age and that destroy the will to function and change. It is the young who can endure the purifying violence that will accompany the revolution, and it is only the young who have the strength to carry the revolution through to the end. But Aflaq is quick to remind his readers that violence and revolution must end in love, for "nationalism is love above everything else." Love will help the Arabs carry out their responsibilities and reestablish Islamic humanism. Furthermore, says Aflaq, all Arabs must marry and procreate to found a new generation of young dedicated to the revolution. All education must likewise be reformed so that "a national Arab stamp will mark all the aspects of intellectual, economic, political, architectural, and artistic life."

The cornerstones of Aflaq's ideology are constitutionalism, democracy, socialism, and nationalism. All of these will exist when the final Arab state evolves, because all are contained in the humanist ideals of Arabism. By constitutionalism, Aflaq means that the Arab governments will have a constitution and a tradition that binds them to act legitimately and responsibly. By democracy, he means that government will be popular and subject to the will of the people. By socialism, he means that Arab government will be responsible for the welfare of all its citizens, and by nationalist, he means that Arab government will be above all one that takes into consideration the history and traditions of the Arab World. Aflaq was realist enough to know that a period would have to pass during which those ideals fell far short of actuality. But he wrote that tyranny and dictatorship would pass from the Arab World because the guiding principles of Arab humanism would conquer all tendencies that restricted human freedom and progress. There would be an invisible hand guiding the Arabs toward perfection of their political, economic, and social institutions.

Al-Alayili, al-Husri, and Aflaq each contributed to Arab self-understanding and development. The charismatic leader that al-Alayili had prescribed as a cure for Arab backwardness appeared in Colonel Nasser of Egypt, who made an indelible imprint on Arab Socialism in that country. Al-Husri's brand of mystical nationalism became a goal of radical governments as they attempted to unify their nations and give their peoples a sense of common purpose. Michael Aflaq's socialism has become the official state ideology of Syria and Iraq.

Revival in the Middle East had come a long way. Early concentration on language and cultural reform produced a language capable of modern discourse. Schools and colleges had been founded, books published; more Arabs could now read and write. Religious concerns had turned men toward the past and had caused them to discover what was best in the Arab tradition. National pride and self-esteem had grown immensely, and with their growth, many Arabs became convinced that they could change their future and improve their lot on earth. Political systems had been borrowed and discarded; new systems had been invented that were more truly Arab and genuinely fitted for use in the Middle East. More men than ever had become aware of the crisis that faced the Arab World, the vicious circle of poverty, ignorance, and backwardness, and were hopeful of doing something about it. All that remained now was for this new maturity to be put into action. By 1950 the Arab World was ripe for radical change. The next stage of the Arab Awakening would see the final winning of independence and the creation of new concerns, as Arabs set about to solve the social and economic problems that had plagued them for centuries.

CHAPTER FOUR

Arab Socialism in Egypt: The First Ten Years

The first Arab socialist revolution happened in Egypt. This event came as a surprise to few, for the situation there had become intolerable in the years following World War II. The king, Farouk, was a playboy who spent large sums on women and luxury. He had lost the respect of his people in 1942 when the British had forced him to carry out their wishes; many felt that the king had become a mere tool of foreign interests. The Wafd Party, that had so long attempted to thwart British power and the power of the king, had become corrupt. It had lost all connection with the idealism and nationalist fervor of its founder, Saad Zaghlul, and seemed incapable of solving Egypt's difficult problems.

No government could calm the turmoil that came to Egypt following the World War. The standard of living fell and thousands were out of work. Regime succeeded regime, some lasting only a matter of days or months. The disorder reached its peak in 1948 and 1949. The pro-British prime minister, Nuqrashi, was murdered by members of the Muslim Brotherhood. Two months later, enemies of the Brotherhood slew Hassan al-Banna, its founder and leader. Acts such as these kept Egyptian society torn apart. Terrorist acts became commonplace. Many students and workers joined the growing factions of the Communist Party; others committed themselves to extreme nationalist groups. It seemed that full-scale civil war might break out at any moment.

The government answered the crisis with repression and tyranny. Thousands of political prisoners were thrown into concentration camps. There, communists mixed with members of the Brotherhood and radical nationalists of all kinds. But the chaos did not subside; even the camps became centers of anti-government activity as the communists and others established study groups to debate Egypt's problems. Indeed, communism itself grew rapidly in popularity for a while; between 1950 and 1952, it reached its peak of strength and influence. It was not that many Egyptians were becoming committed Marxists. About Marxism and its doctrines, most knew little if anything; it was simply that communism seemed to offer a way out of the crisis, a way that had not been tried before.

There was in the background, however, another movement that had not yet tried its strength. A few young army officers, frustrated by their country's weakness and poverty, had formed a group they called the Free Officers. These young men had first been drawn together in 1938 and 1939 when they graduated from the Egyptian military academy. Most were from lower-middle-class backgrounds and would not have been able to attend the academy had not a 1936 law opened the school to all Egyptians and not just the sons of aristocrats.

In 1938 and 1939 they had pledged themselves to work for Egypt's freedom and improvement, but they adopted no definite political and social philosophy. The war years emphasized their hopes for Egypt. The humiliation of the king by the British proved to them that Egypt enjoyed no real independence and was still the pawn of Great Britain. For a while they considered joining al-Banna's Brotherhood, but were fearful that the Brotherhood's rejection of the modern world was unrealistic and unproductive.

But the event that caused the Free Officers to mold themselves into a closely knit, dedicated revolutionary group was the Arab-Israeli War of 1948. Egypt was disastrously defeated in the war, in which many of the young officers fought valiantly. To remove the blame for defeat from himself, King Farouk severely criticized the army and said that it, through its cowardice, was responsible for the defeat. For the Free Officers, this accusation was unpardonable. They knew that Egypt had lost because much of the ammunition and many of the weapons given the army did not work. Guns jammed; grenades failed to go off. The government had bought the cheapest weaponry available and had not bothered to check it for serviceability. The money that should have gone to buy modern rifles and good ammunition had been pocketed by corrupt bureaucrats.

The Free Officers, thus motivated, formed a secret society pledged to overthrow the king. Only men who could be trusted beyond the shadow of a doubt were asked to join, and an elaborate screening process was developed to prevent the disclosure of the group's existence and its plans. Young men of various political persuasions became members. A few were Marxists; some were conservative Muslims. All were united by their nationalist sentiment.

Gamal Abdel Nasser was the natural leader of the Free Officers. It had been Nasser who had brought them together in the late '30s, and it was Nasser now who felt the defeat in the Israeli War most deeply and who was most convinced that something could be done. Nasser was a slim, intense man from middle Egypt, where he had been born the son of a postal clerk. As a youth, he had organized demonstrations against the Balfour Declaration that prepared the way for the establishment of Israel. He read widely in history and biography and knew that Egypt fell far short of what it could be. He had not seriously considered a military career, but when the academy was opened to Egyptians of all classes, he seized upon it as the only hope he had to complete his education and rise in society. Nasser's closest friend among the Free Officers was Abdul Hakim Amer. Anwar al-Sadat was also an early member.

The Free Officers clandestinely distributed pamphlets that attacked the king and the government. They planned to prepare themselves as completely as possible before seizing power and did not expect the coup to occur before 1953 or 1954. But circumstances came to a head before the date they set. In January 1952 widespread rioting hit the country. Much of Cairo went up in flames, and there were nationwide strikes by labor unions. Nasser decided to act quickly, fearing what would happen to Egypt if order and stability were not restored as soon as possible.

From the beginning, Nasser displayed unusual foresight and skill for an army officer inexperienced in government. He realized that no one in Egypt had heard of him or of the Free Officers and knew that there would be little respect or trust for them once they seized power.

Nasser therefore looked for a well-known and beloved leader who would catch the eye of most Egyptians and win their support. He found this figure in General Mohammad Naguib, a man with a reputation for independence. Naguib had resigned his commission in 1942 in protest against the British humiliation of the king. Naguib was honest, direct, and courageous, the very virtues so lacking in King Farouk and other government officials.

With Naguib as the figurehead and Nasser the true power behind the movement, the final date was set for July 1952. Amer, Sadat, and the other Free Officers proved efficient and loyal. The coup went largely as planned; on July 23 the old government was overthrown and the new established. There was no blood spilled in the process and the Egyptian Revolution has gone down in history as the least bloody of modern times. Even the hated and despised king was allowed to leave on his yacht and to keep the fortune he had stored in European banks. A republic was declared with General Naguib in charge. Well-known, moderate politicians were asked to join the government. Throughout the world, commentators complimented Egypt on its peaceful change in government and predicted success for the revolutionaries.

In his *The Philosophy of the Revolution*, published in 1953, Nasser wrote that he and his followers had had no definite idea of the sort of government they hoped to establish after the coup. They realized that some sort of social and economic philosophy would have to emerge if Egypt were to be guided along the path of meaningful change. But they hoped that the philosophy would emerge in practice as they learned the art of government and saw more clearly what Egypt needed.

At first they only vaguely outlined their plans for change. The first item of importance was the destruction of the monarchy. This they achieved quickly and painlessly. But the other items on their agenda were less simple to take care of: they wanted to end all foreign influence in Egypt, down to the last European. They wanted to destroy the power of the great landlords, who flourished at the expense of the peasants, and they wanted to stop the corruption that had plagued public life in Egypt for centuries. What they wanted above all was a strong, respected Egypt that was ruled by a government that could be taken seriously and looked up to by the Egyptian people. They wanted to set an example of revolution for the whole Arab World to follow. The first ten years of the revolution, therefore, can be divided into three phases: first, the securing of political power against all those forces that would work to depose Nasser and bring an end to change; second, the early agrarian and social reforms that laid a basis for the real social revolution that took place after 1961; and, third, the establishment of Egypt as a strong and influential force in world affairs.

The political revolution began immediately. Nasser quickly realized that many elements in Egyptian society wanted nothing so much as to see his movement fail. Older politicians and political notables, many of whom remained in Egypt, were anxious to reassume power. They had the backing of the landholders and wealthy merchants who had been frightened by Nasser's promise of social and economic reform. Likewise, the Muslim Brotherhood looked with distaste upon Nasser and the Free Officers. Although Nasser professed to be a devout believer and worshipped regularly, the Brotherhood found him too secular and threatened to continue their acts of terrorism.

Communists and other leftists also condemned Nasser. They knew nothing of his politics and distrusted his nationalism, feeling that they must act quickly to drive him from power so that Egypt would not become a military dictatorship of the right. Finally, a last threat to Nasser's security became General Naguib himself. The very reasons that had led Nasser to choose the general as the front man of the revolution played against the Free Officers in the long run. The general's popularity was extreme, and he formed a power base all his own. He was not a genuine revolutionary, and, in time, old Wafdist politicians were able to convince him that Nasser was bad for Egypt and that someone should force him from power.

Nasser weathered all these threats. The older politicians were quickly discredited as Nasser began an agrarian-reform program that showed how seriously he took his commitment to eliminate the old social system. Beside Nasser's reforms, the old politicians appeared to be a greedy and corrupt lot who had no interest in the improvement of the country.

The communists and the Muslim Brotherhood were more difficult to deal with. Both had the support of idealistic young people willing to work hard and give their lives to their cause. The communist movement was outlawed, some of its leaders eventually ending up in jail. Since the Communist Party was divided into factions, each warring with the others, the government harassed and threatened the most prominent members of each faction, thereby weakening the movement as a whole.

Nasser had to proceed more cautiously against the Brotherhood, which was much larger and more active than the Communist Party. He did not want to outrage public opinion by handling it with the same repression he had used against the communists. But in 1954 an opportunity came to discredit the members of the Brotherhood with the same efficiency he had used to discredit the old politicians. An attempt was made against Nasser's life, and upon police investigation, the would-be assassin admitted that he had been strongly influenced by the teachings of al-Banna and *Ikhwan*, that is, the Brotherhood. The leaders and activists of the organization were rounded up, and their stores of weapons and explosives confiscated. The organization's power in Egypt was broken for some time.

Finally, Nasser was able to eliminate Naguib as a rival by cleverly showing that the old general, despite his honesty and nationalism, wanted nothing so much as the return of the old system and an end to reform. As Naguib's power grew among certain elements of the population, Nasser countered with threats of resignation. Labor unions and student groups were sent to the streets to demand that Nasser remain. With the possibility of renewed turmoil and civil strife facing the nation, Naguib had to back down. He was placed under house arrest, while Nasser assumed full and open control of the government.

Nasser had hoped at first to give Egypt a republican form of government with freedom of speech and the press. But it had become clear in his dealings with Naguib, the Brotherhood, and the other sources of opposition that such freedoms would be a luxury in Egypt where they seemed to result inevitably in turmoil and chaos. Nasser therefore opted for stability and order, finding it necessary to rule authoritatively. Laws were passed that placed severe restrictions on the press, and powers were granted the police to destroy any potentially subversive movement. Thus one of the first characteristics of the new regime was its concentration of power in the hands of one man, who was responsible only to himself and a few advisers who had helped him rise to power. Authoritarianism, of course, was nothing new in Egyptian society. King Farouk had run a modified police state that had used repression and tyranny to put down opposition. What was new, however, was that the authority and repression exercised by the revolutionary government were set up to oversee change and reform. Farouk's tyranny kept things as they were; Nasser's dictatorship wanted to guide Egypt into a new era.

To counterbalance the power and appeal of other political ideologies, Nasser created his own party and made it the one legal party of Egypt. It was first called the Liberation Rally, and its purpose was to publicize the ideas and activities of the Free Officers or Revolutionary Council. Membership was to be open to all the citizens of Egypt who wanted to work for its goals. Nasser was painfully aware of the political naïveté of the vast majority of his people; he hoped that the Liberation could eradicate some of this ignorance and give the people a feeling that they were shaping their own destiny.

In 1956, when the government proclaimed its first constitution, the Liberation Rally was changed to the National Union. The Union was given a pyramid structure, with the Free Officers at the top and successive layers of officials and party members all the way down to the village and local level. Workers and peasants were to have a say in the party and be recognized as essential members at all levels of party government. On one hand, the Union was to permit the expression of ideas and grievances from below to rise to the top; on the other hand, the Union was so organized that the Free Officers had total control and could exercise power efficiently in the most remote areas of the country.

The Union was to have several duties. First of all it had to weed out all candidates for office who could not be trusted to express the opinions of the Free Officers. Those of the far right, such as the members of the Brotherhood, or of the far left, such as the communists, were to be discarded. A problem arose when it became apparent that many of those rising to power in the National Union were men who had had political experience under the old regime and who often were not dedicated to the revolution. But Nasser, ever watchful, was quick to discover this and take measures to control the power of these potentially subversive politicians.

A second duty of the National Union was to instill selflessness and honesty in government officials. Corruption and greed were to be done away with. The Union was to condemn and hold up for contempt all officials who had used their office for personal advancement; the time-honored tradition of winking at the pocketing of public money was to be stopped. The Union, too, was to propagandize the positive goals of the new government. It was constantly to condemn every aspect of the old order and show that the Free Officers stood for social justice, progress, and independence.

With the repression of political opposition and the creation of the National Union, Nasser's efforts at political revolution during the first ten years of his regime came to an end. The security of his government had been maintained and most threats silenced. Yet Nasser had not limited his activity to staying in power, as dictators of less imagination and ability would have done. From the very beginning, his eye had been on reform as well as on power, and from the beginning he had acted upon his desire for reform.

The first social and economic reform to be undertaken was agrarian. Nasser himself and others among the Free Officers had lived close to the peasant and knew that his fate was terrible and unrelieved. Landowners had lived off the peasantry for centuries, yet had enjoyed all the political, social, and economic prestige that Egypt had to offer. By destroying the enormous estates that gave a few great wealth, Nasser knew that he was killing two birds with one stone. He gained the support of the peasantry and he brought an end to the power of the old aristocracy.

The first reform came in September 1952. It limited the size of all landholdings to two hundred feddans (a feddan is equal to 1.038 acres). An extra hundred feddans were granted if the landowner had two or more children to support. The land taken by the government from all estates above two hundred feddans was to be divided among the landless in lots of two to five feddans. Some compensation was granted to the landholders who lost land. But since this compensation was based on the tax they had paid during the old regime, the radical government found it necessary to pay out little compensation —the landholders had too often avoided paying heavy taxes and had often bribed officials so that they had to pay no taxes at all. Only one great landholder tried to resist the agrarian reform law by force. A Bedouin chieftain from southern Egypt attempted to thwart the land distribution in his own area by mustering his old tribal forces in a war against the new government. He was not successful, however, and was tried and sentenced to life imprisonment.

The government also attacked the problem of peasant debt. A severe limitation was placed on the amount of rent that could be charged to peasants who rented land. Contracts were to be in writing, so that those who rented land might not take advantage of peasants who rented from them. For the first time, many peasants knew exactly what their relation to landowners was. The 1952 agrarian laws likewise required that peasants be paid a minimum wage so that the extreme poverty of many agricultural workers who owned no land might be alleviated. Not all these measures were carried out fully in the months and years following their announcement. The government bureaucracy was still too small and inefficient to oversee all reform. Yet many millions of Egyptians did benefit, and for the first time meaningful change had come to Egyptian society.

To prevent the falling off of agricultural production that might have come when land formerly under one owner was distributed among a number of owners, the government created cooperatives and expanded earlier cooperatives that had been set up under the old regime. These cooperatives saw that one crop was produced over large areas, but that the produce of each separate holding was kept apart and the name of the owner used to identify his crop. In that way, crop production was maintained at a high level, but each new landowner was given a sense of personal ownership and achievement.

The cooperatives likewise arranged for the distribution of fertilizer, seed, machinery, and other modern agricultural materials. By the early '60s, the cooperatives had been expanded to provide for systems of transportation to get the produce to market so that each small farmer received a return on his crop. Graduates of agricultural schools were sent to each cooperative to introduce modern techniques of plant care and animal husbandry. Crop rotation was introduced on a systematic basis—in 1956, for instance, triennial rotation was made compulsory in areas under the land-reform laws.

In the late '50s and early '60s, the government decided to gradually extend the cooperative program to the whole country. A village in the Nile Delta was chosen as an example to skeptical peasants to show what could be accomplished. The experimental village was a success, and many conservative peasants became convinced that cooperatives were a good idea.

The industrial and urban economic policy of the Nasser government was at first far more cautious than its agrarian policy. The old regime had collected a number of debts to Western countries before Nasser seized power, and the Free Officers felt that it was best not to repudiate these debts outright, but to develop a conservative and prudent economic program that would inspire respect in the West and lead to investment and loans by Western governments and private corporations.

But it soon became apparent that most Western investors were very wary of Nasser and the Free Officers. No money was forthcoming and an impatient Nasser found it necessary to find other sources to support his plans for reform and progress. In 1956 Nasser nationalized the foreign enterprises operating in Egypt. He declared the Suez Canal to be Egyptian property and asked the British to leave. When Britain and France invaded Egypt at the time of the second Arab-Israeli War, he completed his nationalizations and began to set up government agencies to supervise the new money and acquisitions. All French and English banks and insurance companies had been seized, and Nasser hoped that they would provide a basis for Egyptian industrial expansion. A five-year plan—modeled on the plans for industrial growth developed in the Soviet Union—was announced in 1958. Negotiations with the Soviet Union had resulted in a promise to build the Aswan Dam in southern Egypt, a dam that would provide the electric power necessary to run new industry and supply water for irrigation.

Nasser also concentrated on the improvement of the Egyptian armed forces. Training was improved and modern weapons obtained from Russia, Czechoslovakia, and other communist countries. The defeat in 1948 and again in 1956 was not forgotten, nor was the promise to build an Egypt that was strong and powerful. Defense remained the largest single expenditure; the military was close to Nasser's heart and an essential part of his plans for Egypt. He looked upon its support as a guarantee of his revolution's security, and felt it to be the single most important force in Egyptian society leading to modernization.

Nasser's most dramatic achievements in the first ten years of his government, however, and the achievements that brought him world-wide fame, were not his programs of agrarian and industrial reform or his improvement of the army. They were rather his activities in the field of foreign policy. Critics were later to say that Nasser had entered foreign affairs because of the failure of his domestic revolution, that when the problems of social and economic change became too great, he became interested in the more flamboyant field of international affairs to distract the people of Egypt from their poverty and misery which he found he could not alleviate.

But such criticisms are largely unfair to Nassar. Whatever domestic program he might have followed, Nasser could not have turned Egypt away from her chronic poverty and backwardness overnight. Years would pass before Egyptian society and economy could be meaningfully improved, and during that time Nasser could not have ignored the rest of the world. Indeed, his foreign policy was part of the total program of reform he envisioned. For a genuine revolution to take place, he felt that it was necessary for Egypt's relationship with other nations to be altered. If Egypt were to be strong and independent, its role in world affairs would have to be dramatically changed.

In *The Philosophy of the Revolution*, Nasser wrote that the days of Egypt's isolation were over. He outlined three general areas or circles of responsibility that Egypt would have to assume as an independent nation. The first of the three areas was the Arab World. Egypt, as a free and revolutionary country, had to assume leadership in the Arab struggle for independence. Egypt could not rest on its own success, for unless the whole Arab World were freed from colonialism and exploitation, Egypt would be continually threatened.

The next area or circle of Egypt's responsibility was Africa. Here, Nasser pointed out, there were millions of blacks subjugated by a small number of whites. Egypt would have to join the struggle for freedom throughout Africa, for Egypt was a part of Africa just as she was a part of the Arab World. Finally, the third circle of Egyptian responsibility was the Muslim World as a whole—the hundreds of millions of people in Pakistan, Indonesia, and elsewhere in Asia—who were still under the yoke of colonialism and backwardness. These fellow Muslims likewise needed Egypt's example and inspiration.

What Nasser outlined in theory, he tried to carry out in practice. His first concern was to drive the British from Egypt and to eliminate all foreign influence that remained. His second was to become a leader of the neutral, unaligned nations—the countries that supported neither the West nor the communists. In the process of attaining both goals, he made tremendous mistakes, but he also was largely successful. What no critic can deny is that Nasser had made Egypt into a nation whose interests were known throughout the world.

Nasser proceeded against the British at first with caution and deliberation. The British had immediately withdrawn support after the coup, fearing that the Free Officers were totally anti-British. Negotiations between Nasser and the British government followed and ended in a treaty whereby the British promised to withdraw eventually. Many nationalists accused Nasser of selling out and of making the same indefinite agreements that earlier governments had made. Nasser himself disliked the arrangements, and, in 1956, took the step that would sever Egypt's tie with its colonial past forever. He nationalized the Suez Canal and ordered the British army to leave its bases immediately.

British and French troops invaded Egypt to "restore order" and return the canal to European ownership. But Nasser had played his cards right. World opinion was overwhelmingly against the British and the French. The United States joined the Soviet Union and scores of other countries in condemning the invasion and supporting the Egyptians. Britain and France were forced to withdraw and to accept the canal's loss. Nasser was triumphant in Egypt and throughout the Arab World. For the first time an Arab had stood up to the West and had emerged successful.

In his relations with the Soviet Union and the United States, Nasser tried to forge new instruments of negotiation and strength. He considered himself sincerely neutral and hoped to balance one superpower against the other. In 1955 he received a shipment of arms from Czechoslovakia. When the United States protested, he refused to back down. Even a boycott by the United States failed to turn Nasser's position. When America refused to finance the Aswan Dam project, a giant construction designed to dam the Nile River, Nasser obtained a loan from Russia, as well as other monetary and military help. Later, the American government began to reconsider giving aid.

Indeed, Nasser had played East against West and had gained many benefits from both. If at times Egypt seemed leaning toward the Soviet Union, this was acceptable to him, for he felt that Egypt had too long depended entirely on the West.

As Nasser gained fame for his stands against the West, his pre-eminence in the Third World grew. In 1955 he went to the Bandung Conference of unallied nations on the island of Java in Indonesia. Here he talked with Chou En-lai, the Chinese communist, and to other Third World leaders. He was treated as an equal by men he had long respected; he came away from the conference with the feeling that he could rise to the position of one of the two or three most powerful figures in the Third World. The Bandung Conference had underlined his belief that neutralism was possible and that it was a movement essential to world order and peace.

Nasser turned Egypt into a center for African nationalist and revolutionary movements. From 1954 he supported various groups, offering them a headquarters in Cairo and money to finance their work. Likewise, Radio Cairo broadcasted regularly to the nations of Africa, preaching rebellion and revolution against colonial masters. But Egypt's most important role was in the Arab World itself. He welcomed Algerian freedom fighters to Cairo and provided them with money and support. When the Algerian Revolution broke out in 1954, he was quick to aid the revolutionaries and offered Egypt as a place to train guerrilla fighters. Algerian leaders often found a refuge in Egypt, and Nasser bombarded North Africa with propaganda in support of the Algerian rebels.

Nasser's popularity and fame helped topple governments in Syria and Iraq. Iraqi revolutionaries overthrew the conservative dictator, Nuri al-Said, hoping to institute Nasser-like reforms in their country. In Syria young army officers influenced by Michael Aflaq's Arab Socialism thought that unity between Egypt and Syria might create a great Arab revolutionary movement that would alter the Middle East entirely. Indeed, Michael Aflaq traveled to Cairo himself and talked with Nasser about the union.

Nasser was enthusiastic, and in 1958 the creation of the United Arab Republic was announced. Thousands of Egyptian officials traveled to Syria to oversee reform, to conduct the expropriation of land and the nationalization of foreign concerns. But the Syrian adventure was one of Nasser's great mistakes. No sooner had Egyptian officials entered Syria than the Syrians became fearful that their national identity and freedom were being destroyed. They resented what they felt to be Egyptian arrogance and soon wanted Nasser's administrators out of their country. By 1961 the experiment was called a failure and the two countries went their separate ways.

Nasser had likewise failed in his relation with Israel during the first ten years of his regime. Always violently anti-Israel, he had vowed to destroy the country and return the land to the Palestinian Arabs who had been forced out when the Jewish State was created. Nasser hoped to wage a successful war against the Israelis, a war that would erase the humiliation caused by the defeat of 1948. But Nasser's defeat in the Arab-Israeli War of 1956 was just as pronounced as the earlier defeat had been, and he was only able to save his regime because of his success in taking the Suez Canal.

By the end of the first decade of Nasser's rule, the general characteristics of Arab Socialism in Egypt had been decided, although the country could not yet be classified as a socialist country. Its most pronounced characteristic thus far was its authoritarianism. Decisions were made at the top by a small, elite group of former and active army officers. A "cult of personality" had been created with Nasser as the central, charismatic figure of the revolution. A party structure—the National Union—had been established throughout the land to implement the decisions made by Nasser and his followers. The heavy hand of the government was felt by all who dared oppose the rulers. No party was tolerated except the party that reflected the opinions of the leaders; there was no freedom of the press or of speech. The ruling elite believed that it knew what was best for Egypt, and that it alone should be permitted to guide the country in its transformation to a more just and stable society. Nasser and his followers knew that if they did not rule authoritatively, Egypt would again degenerate into anarchy, and the gains of the revolution would be lost.

The other characteristics of the new regime were less negative. It had shown a serious and committed desire for reform. It had developed a pragmatic attitude toward reform, adopting policy as it felt it was needed. In the first ten years of Nasser's rule, corruption among officials declined perceptibly. Nasser himself was a man of principle and never succumbed to the lure of wealth or luxury that his position of power might have brought. Likewise, the government had taken definitive steps for the reorganization of the social and economic structures of Egypt: land had been seized and distributed, industries had been nationalized. If the socialist transformation of the country was far from complete, Nasser and the Free Officers had shown a preference for pragmatic government planning and for public owner-ship of significant amounts of property—both central features of a socialist system. And Nasser had definitely rejected capitalism as exploitive and imperialistic.

Finally, Egypt's new regime showed that it favored an aggressive and experimental foreign policy, one that would not be tied to the weakness and obsequiousness of the past. Such a foreign policy was bound to be clumsy and awkward as it exercised power for the first time. Yet it reflected the basic underlying feature of all the efforts taken by Nasser's government—the nationalism that had caused Nasser and the Free Officers to seize power in the first place. This nationalism was likewise to guide Nasser as he took Egypt through the second, and more radical, decade of its revolution.

CHAPTER FIVE

Socialism in Egypt: The Second Ten Years

The failure of the union with Syria was a traumatic setback for
Nasser. He believed that capitalist and conservative elements in
Syrian society had organized the opposition to Egypt and to socialism; he feared that the same reactionary elements might seize control
in his own country and undo the work of the past ten years. He therefore speeded up the rate of the revolution and initiated a series of
reforms that transformed Egypt into an Arab socialist state.

These reforms were more systematic and better planned than the
reforms of the early '50s. In 1962 a thirty-thousand word document
was published that outlined Nasser's hopes for Egypt and discussed
the sort of social and economic reform that was being undertaken.
The National Charter, as this document was called, flatly stated that
the "objectives which are a true expression of Arab national conscience" were "Freedom, Socialism and Unity." Freedom was
described simply as "freedom of the country and freedom of the citizen." Unity was said to refer to the solidarity of the nation, both spir-
itually and physically. It was:

> the popular call for the restoration of the natural order
> of the nation, torn apart by its enemies against its own
> will and interests, and the peaceful endeavor to pro-
> mote this unity and finally its unanimous acceptance as a
> crowning achievement.

Socialism, the third element that truly expressed the Arab conscience according to the National Charter, was called both an end and a means—both a goal to strive for and a means that would help Egypt to achieve the goals of unity and freedom. Socialism was "sufficiency and justice," sufficiency being the strength and ability to function alone, without the aid of wealthier and stronger nations, while justice was the equal distribution of property and opportunity, the abolition of all artificial distinctions between individuals.

The National Charter assumed that true democracy would be achieved through socialism. "Political democracy cannot be separated from social democracy," it said, assuming that capitalist systems of Western democracies produced inequities and injustices that prevented true democracy. Every citizen could be regarded as genuinely free only when the state had given him these three guarantees:

(a) he should be free from all exploitation in all its forms;
(b) he should enjoy an equal opportunity with his fellow citizens to enjoy a fair share of the national wealth;
(c) his mind should be free from all anxiety likely to undermine his future security.

It was the aim of the revolutionary government to secure these three freedoms for every Egyptian.

The National Charter was also careful to define its doctrine of socialism as "scientific socialism." By this it meant that all "the experience of modern science" should be used in the development of the social and economic plan to guide the socialist transformation. Economic wisdom and expertise, gathered from the experience of other socialist nations, would regulate the Egyptian economy and society. President Nasser had come to realize that Egypt needed modern experts, technicians, and others who understood the complexity of modernization and government planning. The phrase "scientific socialism" was his recognition of the intricacies and difficulties of socialism.

The National Charter was not fated to exist only on paper. Even before its aims were presented to the public, the government had initiated a new series of reforms. In July 1961 the maximum size of an estate was reduced from two hundred feddans to one hundred. Landholders were allowed until 1970 to sell all land they held in excess of the new limit; land not sold was to be expropriated. The government, of course, ordered that prices on land would be low and within easy reach of the poor. In 1962 all land held by foreigners was expropriated and placed in the pool of land being distributed among the landless.

The supervised cooperatives that had proved so successful in the '50s were expanded and plans were made to place the whole country under such organizations. Plans were also made to extend electrical power and make it available in all rural areas; new irrigation schemes were presented to the nation that would put new land under cultivation. The Aswan High Dam, completed in the mid-'60s, provided the energy and water that made these projects possible.

The National Charter recognized the central importance of agriculture to the country. It argued that crop production and rural well-being were essential to a strong nation, and that Egypt had to be put on a firm agricultural basis before expansion could take place in the rest of the economy. But the National Charter and the period of reforms beginning in 1961 by no means ignored industry and other aspects of the economy. In February 1960 the large private Egyptian banks, the Bank Misr and the National Bank of Egypt, were nationalized. In June the press that had long endured repression was seized and made government property, as was the Cairo bus system.

In June and July of 1961 the government appropriated the entire import trade of the country and a sizable portion of the export trade. Cotton, Egypt's most important export, was placed under government control and supervision. All other banks and insurance companies were likewise taken over and several hundred industries and other commercial enterprises were either totally nationalized or partially seized by the government. In a few short months the whole complexion of Egyptian society had been changed, but the transformation was yet far from complete.

Severe restrictions were placed on personal wealth. A heavy income tax was introduced that limited personal income to $18,000 or below. Limitations were made on the number of shares an individual could own in any company, so that no one could assert undue influence on industry or trade. In a blow aimed at destroying the wealthy merchants and other members of the upper middle class, the government sequestered the wealth and property of Egypt's six hundred wealthiest families, many of whom were Jews or Coptic Christians and had long feared the Arab nationalism of the government.

If the wealthier and better off suffered from the new laws, the worker often found them beneficial. A policy of public sharing of profits made in industry was introduced. Factories and other businesses were instructed that 25 percent of their profits were to be divided among the workers in the form of cash, increased benefits, and in other ways. The workers received the first cash payments under the new plan in 1962.

New laws likewise organized factories into committees in which workers had a say. The number of working hours was reduced to forty-two, and the minimum wage increased. Worker benefits in the form of old-age pensions, disability and dependent insurance were increased and improved, as they continued to be throughout the '60s. Further nationalization of private industries and concerns took place in 1963 and 1964, often in agriculturally related firms such as rice and flour mills, bakeries, and river transport systems.

In July 1960 the first five-year plan of 1958 was discarded and a new one instituted. A second five-year plan was begun in 1965. The aim of the two plans was to double the national income by 1970. In the plans, government investment was to be heaviest in industry and electricity, the two facets of Egyptian life most painfully short of the standards of modern, technological societies such as Japan or the United States.

The idea behind the plans was to transform Egypt into a nation that enjoyed all the benefits of a highly developed economy: a surplus of consumer goods, substantial employment, and a high standard of living. The plans sought to diversify the economy and reduce the reliance on one crop—cotton—to bring money to the country. Diversification meant economic security in times the cotton crop might fail or when prices on the world market might fall. Government investment was thus made in television plants and in factories that produced a variety of products such as insecticides, refrigerators, bicycles, and electrical supplies. Arrangements were made with foreign companies to send already manufactured parts to Egypt to be assembled by Egyptian workers. During the first five-year plan, industrial growth was impressive, and the gross national product increased by more than 6 percent each year, a respectable achievement. The economy had grown fast enough to outstrip the population growth. In some areas, such as the construction of new buildings, the government had exceeded the estimates given in the plan. There was much rejoicing, and hopes were raised that the future boded well for Egypt.

Nasser likewise used the early '60s as a period of consolidation and improvement of Egypt's one-party political system. The National Union had never been effective, because no one had ever been clear on what its make-up and purpose were to be. After the Union had been put into effect in 1957 and 1958, it had been repeatedly modified as new ideas presented themselves. In this uncertainty, Nasser had received criticisms that he was not really interested in hearing the opinions of the masses of people and that he had no desire to consult the popular will.

Nasser was sensitive to such attacks, and, although he had no desire to relinquish his control of the revolution, he genuinely wanted to create institutions that would someday evolve into a more democratic system, where many opinions found expression. The National Charter set the goals of Egyptian democracy to be the rule of the whole people:

> *Political democracy cannot exist under the domination of any one class. Democracy means, literally, the domination and sovereignty of the people—the whole people.*

From Marxism, Nasser had learned that "the political system in any state is only a reflection of the interests controlling the economic system," as he wrote in the Charter, and it was therefore important to him that Egypt's political system show that the poor and underprivileged now played an important part in shaping the country's destiny.

The National Charter changed the name of the National Union to the Arab Socialist Union. The basic unit of the Arab Socialist Union were the cells established in the villages of rural Egypt and in the factories, companies, government agencies, and commercial establishments of the cities. Each group elected a twenty-man committee that held office for two years and met twice a month. All the members of each cell were to meet every four months. Each committee elected two of its members to represent it on the next highest committee at the district level. The district committee was to select a number of men from its own members to oversee the district. The district committee in turn elected officials to a higher committee, and so on, until the nationwide committee was formed. At all levels, measures were taken to assure representation of many interest groups —the army, women, the police force, and so on.

Fully half the seats on each level—local, district, national—were to be held by workers and farmers. As the National Charter pointed out, the vast majority of Egyptians were either workers or farmers who had never enjoyed representation of any sort in Egyptian government. Under the National Union no provision had been made to assure their participation. A worker was defined as anyone who belonged to a union, while a farmer was anyone who held less than twenty-five feddans of land. One out of every two committee members of the Arab Socialist Union was to come from these groups.

In addition to the ASU, Nasser drew up plans for a national parliament that would have representatives from the whole of Egypt. In early 1964 he announced the creation of the National Assembly. It was to have three hundred and fifty members—two each from one hundred and seventy-five districts. As in the case of ASU membership, one representative from each district was to be a farmer or worker. All delegates had to be able to read and write and had to be members of the Arab Socialist Union. The first elections for the National Assembly were held in March, and for a country that had experienced nothing but corrupt elections for decades, they went well. Corruption and the buying of office were far less than they had been in any election under the old government. Although only members of the one political party were allowed to run, many people took great interest in the outcome and worked to make the election meaningful. Perhaps no better indication of the change that had overcome Egypt exists than the fact that twenty-eight women were running for office.

The power granted the Assembly was one of consideration and approval of the laws, tax system, and other facets of government established by Nasser and his Revolutionary Council. Nasser told the Assembly after it convened that it was to share his executive power. His government would be responsible to the Assembly, and any delegate could call a member of the government up short for questioning. The Assembly was reminded, however, that it was to act responsibly and was not to question government policy merely as a means to assert its own power.

Government reorganization in the early '60s was not limited to economic and political considerations. A vast expansion of state activity took place in the areas of welfare and other public services. The raising of the Egyptian health standards was of primary concern. The National Charter had made its position on medicine clear:

> *The right of each citizen to medical care, whether treatment or medicine, should not be a commodity for sale or purchase. It should be a guaranteed right independent of any price. Medical care should be within the reach of every citizen, in every part of the country, and under easy conditions. Health insurance must be extended to cover all citizens.*

The government realized that it would have to assume the primary responsibility for the expansion and improvement of medical care and facilities. In a poor country like Egypt, there was simply no private individual or institution wealthy enough to finance the building of hospitals and clinics.

The education of doctors and other medical personnel was encouraged and financed. Indeed, the most popular profession today among Egyptian students is medicine. The number of hospital beds was vastly increased, and Egypt soon became one of the most advanced of the undeveloped countries as to the availability of medical care. The 1964–65 budget alone provided for three new central hospitals, five general hospitals, two mental disease centers, six infant welfare clinics, three centers dealing with chest and respiratory ailments, and a clinic for infantile paralysis. The government met the expenses through careful planning and use of loans from foreign countries.

The level of health in the countryside was improved. Centers were set up in villages to help educate people in cleanliness and simple hygiene. In one of the most important developments, it was announced in 1966 that the entire rural population had access to pure water—seventeen million people, as opposed to two million at the time of the revolution.

In the '60s, the government began to address itself to one of Egypt's most severe problems for the first time. For years Nasser had ignored the problem of population and had rejected the idea of birth control or of a limit to population expansion. He feared that birth control would limit the number of men available to the army, but he also felt that birth control was a policy urged by the rich Western nations to limit the size and strength of other nations. Furthermore, he knew that most Egyptian males prided themselves on the size of their families, and that small families were considered an insult to masculine standards.

But by 1961 the population crisis had become severe. Egypt's population was increasing at a million a year, and these million new mouths had to be fed. Nasser feared that what gains might be made through economic and agricultural reform would be wiped out by the unchecked population growth. Indeed, an American consulting firm, after a thorough analysis of Egyptian society, had warned the Egyptian leader that given the enormous increase in the number of people, Egypt could complete its five-year plans successfully in all details and with no failures and still only break even as far as economic growth and progress were concerned.

The National Charter succinctly outlined the problem:

> *The increase constitutes the most dangerous obstacle that faces the Egyptian people in their drive towards raising the levels of income and production in an effective and efficient way . . . family planning deserves the most sincere efforts supported by modern scientific methods . . . regardless of the effects which may result from the experiment.*

In keeping with this directive, the government began the establishment of birth-control clinics, and by 1966 four hundred and fifteen such clinics had been created in all parts of Egypt. Already some drop in the birthrate is noted, but significant change will take time.

The birth-control program encountered numerous difficulties, as can best be illustrated by a story connected with the efforts to change the attitude of the average Egyptian toward large families. A poster was made and put up in various places throughout the country. It had two pictures on it; one of a small family, a mother, father, and a single child, a daughter. The small family was living in a comfortable apartment and was obviously enjoying economic well-being and security. The other picture showed a large family. The father looked worried and worn out from trying to support his many children. The mother looked exhausted from repeated childbirth; the children were poor and hungry.

The poster was intended to show the average Egyptian that he could improve his standard of living by limiting the size of his family. But many Egyptians, seeing the poster, reacted sharply in a different way. They condemned the father of the small family for not having a son—in traditional Islamic societies men often divorce women who bear them only daughters. They condemned him for not having as many children as God permitted him, but they reserved their greatest condemnation for the woman of the small family who had forsaken her duty to have children and was living in luxury and pleasure.

On the other hand, these Egyptians praised the father and mother of the large family for their unselfishness and for their dutifulness in carrying out Allah's commands and in enriching the fatherland with sons. Although the attitude toward birth control and change in general has altered since the poster was displayed, the story underlines the problem the government faces in transforming the cast of mind of the average Egyptian and the difficulty of developing attitudes compatible with modernization and progress.

Other social problems caused by tradition and custom were also attacked. Under old Islamic law and practice, husbands enjoyed the right of easy divorce if their wives did not please them. Men were permitted up to four wives at one time, and although this practice was not as common in Egypt as in other Arab lands, it had still led to abuses. The problem underlying divorce and polygamy was the inferior and degraded status of women. One half the population was held to be unworthy of the rights granted to the other half; the Koran itself sanctioned this attitude by repeatedly calling women "one step lower than men."

Clearly, no modern society could transform and improve its condition if half its people were held in contempt and kept ignorant. The National Charter recognized this fact:

Woman must be regarded as equal to man and she must

therefore shed the remaining shackles that impede her free movement, so that she may play a constructive and profoundly important part in shaping the life of the country.

Educational opportunities were therefore extended to women. Larger numbers of girls were admitted to grammar and high schools. In the '60s, the first women doctors were granted their degrees. Women became active in the press, parliament, and in factories, schools, and offices. In 1962 Dr. Hikmat Abou Zeid became the first woman minister in the government, and by 1964 women had been appointed as judges, where they would be exercising decisions over males. But progress for women was uneven, and reporters who interviewed Nasser and other members of the Revolutionary Council discovered that the wives of the leaders never spoke and often sat in the next room, in the traditional Muslim manner, taking no part in the interview and the discussion among the males.

Education in general was transformed by the changes instituted in the early '60s. In 1961 al-Azhar University, an old center of Muslim learning, was modernized by the addition of new faculties of medicine, science, and engineering. New grammar schools were built, and teacher education was expanded so that the new schools would be adequately staffed. The government had come to realize that if socialism was going to work in Egypt, a literate and trained populace was essential.

Coupled with the expansion of education was a growth in the propaganda arm of the government. The revolutionary leaders had long been active propagandists, but in the early '60s, more systematic efforts were made to control public opinion. The press was completely nationalized in 1960. In the same year the government inaugurated the first television stations, which soon became the most efficient network in the Arab World. Book publishing was likewise expanded under government supervision, and writers and artists were granted subsidies to support them in their work. The end result, of course, was that the government's message loomed ever larger before the Egyptian public. Television and newspapers presented Nasser's ideas and innovations; movies tried to win sympathy for the revolution. Likewise, books and works of art reflected what was held acceptable by government censors, and there was no room for contrary viewpoints.

The years between 1960 and 1965 were kind to the Egyptian revolutionary movement. The first five-year plan was going well and significant reforms were taking place in all parts of society. The second five-year plan, however, went badly from the beginning. The primary reason was that the sources of foreign money dried up. Western governments and investors had grown to fear Egypt once again; nationalizations threatened, at any time, to turn foreign money and property over to the state without compensation. Nasser attempted to assure the foreigners that the era of nationalizations was over after the early '60s and that Egyptian society had returned to a period of stability, but he was not convincing. Egypt's credit dried up and the foreign sources of money looked elsewhere for places to invest.

The effect on Egypt was startling and immediate. New factories closed down because raw materials could not be obtained. Money became scarce, and the consumer goods that had become more common in Egyptian stores began to disappear. In a hasty and ill-considered move, Nasser stopped payment on Egypt's large loan from the International Monetary Fund. The Fund had demanded that Egypt devalue her currency to meet her current crisis; Nasser felt that these demands were an insult to Egyptian independence and decided to try to weather the crisis alone.

A program of austerity was initiated, the socialist government claiming that hardship would be visited on all citizens equally. Imports were restricted severely, especially raw materials and capital goods, so there would no longer be a drain on the treasury. A slump in the rate of economic growth followed, the average annual growth rate falling from 6 percent to 2½ percent. The second five-year plan was changed to a seven-year plan, the first two years of which were to be "years of consolidation."

But the few advances that were made during the years of consolidation were wiped out by the Arab-Israeli War of 1967. Nasser was soundly defeated. Egypt lost the Suez Canal, which was closed to travel, and the revenue from the canal that had been an important part of Egypt's income came to an end. The Sinai Peninsula was likewise lost, along with oil fields that had just begun opening there. Indeed, the crisis was so severe that Nasser threatened to resign When popular opinion demanded that he remain in power, he reorganized his cabinet and began a thorough reassessment of the socialist measures that had been taken in the early '60s.

First, the government took serious steps to establish Egypt's credit by beginning to repay debts that had been repudiated or simply allowed to go unpaid. It was hoped that this would bring in money from the cautious Western investors who had been frightened away. Plans were made to build a pipeline from the Red to the Mediterranean Sea to carry oil from the Arabian Peninsula that would have been carried on ships through the canal. Egypt hoped that revenue from this pipeline would help replace that lost when the canal was closed. Also, investigation had turned up oil deposits along the Red Sea and in western Egypt, near the Libyan border, as well as deposits of natural gas in the Nile Delta. Foreign companies expressed an interest in permission to develop these resources. Iron ore deposits that had raised the government's hopes for Egyptian steel production were to be exploited by the state.

After the reestablishment of credit, a second reassessment that took place after 1967 was over the degree of socialization that was best for the country. How much of a private sector should remain beside the government-owned areas of the economy? Nasser realized that part of the lag in growth that had begun in 1965 was due to overnationalization: Egypt simply did not have the money and capital to finance broad economic reforms. This money had to come from somewhere; it could not be manufactured from nothing. Nasser had never favored total state ownership, but he had never decided the point at which the state should stop and private enterprise begin. When publicly financed construction came to an end following the 1967 war, private companies were allowed to do most of the new construction needed in the country; expansion of other private business continued. Nasser hoped that this mixed economy would prove vital and progressive, but he warned the private corporations and businesses that they would never be permitted to exploit or take advantage of Egyptian workers.

The problem of worker incentives also came up for assessment. Since the reforms of the early '60s, workers had enjoyed secure positions and so much power that it was a rare manager or employer that could fire or threaten a lazy, incompetent man. The problem was simple: in a country that wanted increased production to raise the standard of living, how could a worker be inspired to be efficient and productive without impinging on his right to a job? There was no easy solution. Nasser, however, decided against higher salaries and increased opportunities for advancement. Rather, he urged the increased distribution of profits among lower income workers, hoping thereby to raise their standard of living and working incentive.

A last area of reassessment was the bureaucracy. The bureaucracy had rapidly expanded as socialization called for more and more agencies and officials to oversee the new socialist laws and supervise expropriated property. But few trained individuals were available to run and work in such important agencies, and often the new bureaucracy bogged down in inefficiency. Often the new bureaucracies were expanded simply to give work to unemployed men who could find work nowhere else.

Corruption too was a problem of the new bureaucracy. As government wealth and power grew, the opportunity for personal enrichment increased. Not all government administrators had the honesty of a Nasser, and many pocketed money that came through their departments. The bureaucratic class threatened to become a new upper class that exploited the masses and enjoyed a way of life superior to that available to the average worker. The problems of the bureaucracy bothered Nasser greatly, and he hoped that the Arab Socialist Union would emerge as an effective overseer and judge of bureaucratic corruption and inefficiency.

The foreign policy of the last ten years of the Nasser government lacked the drama and fireworks of the first decade. Nasser still exercised the role of leadership among Third World nations, but more and more his energies were concentrated on the Arab World. He hoped to carry the revolution to other countries in the Middle East and establish his influence there. One after another, however, these efforts failed, often disastrously, and distracted from the popularity Nasserism had enjoyed in the first decade of its existence.

The '60s had opened with the failure of the union with Syria. The Syrians had asked the Egyptians to leave because they felt the Egyptians were trampling on Syrian national rights. Egyptian influence in Algeria declined for much the same reason. Nasser had granted aid to the rebels in their struggle against France, but the rebels had come to resent Egyptian aid because of the demands and requirements placed on it. The Algerians did not wish to be dictated to by the Egyptians, and when success came in 1962, with the withdrawal of the French, they wanted to have nothing to do with Egypt or Nasser. Indeed, the Algerian revolutionaries announced that their socialism would avoid the cult of personality and strong-man rule they felt had corrupted Egypt's revolution.

But more serious than Egypt's failure with Syria or Algeria was its involvement in Yemen. In the late summer of 1962 a group of young Yemeni army officers, who admired Nasser, rebelled against the new ruler of their country, the Imam Badr, who had just succeeded his father. The rebellion was led by Brigadier Abdullah el-Sallal, who immediately seized the chief towns of Yemen and drove the new Imam into the mountains. A civil war followed as royalist fought republican.

Saudi Arabia came to the support of Imam Badr and his followers, while Egypt supported the rebels. Nasser poured money, weapons, ammunition, and Egyptian soldiers into the war. At one time, fifty thousand Egyptian troops were there, but no decisive battle could be won. Yemen became Egypt's Vietnam, absorbing money and men that should have been at home helping to rebuild the country. Nasser himself came to recognize the venture as a total failure and was relieved when a treaty in 1967 established a coalition government in Yemen. At a high price, he had discovered that it was difficult to transport revolution.

The most disastrous of Nasser's efforts, however, was the third Arab-Israeli War of June 1967. It took the Israelis only seven days to defeat soundly and decisively the army that Nasser had spent years equipping and training. The 1967 war covered the army with shame; Egyptian soldiers abandoned the latest Soviet tanks and other equipment to flee Israeli attacks. Much land was lost, and Nasser himself was covered with humiliation.

The Arab defeat helped to exacerbate what had been happening for some time. To replace the arms and ammunition lost in the war, Nasser relied ever more heavily on the Soviet Union. The days of strict neutrality were over; Soviet advisers and military personnel entered the country in larger numbers. Pessimistic observers felt that it was only a matter of time before Egypt became a Russian satellite.

In the fall of 1970, however, Nasser died of a heart attack. He had been suffering from diabetes since the '50s and had vastly overworked himself during the period of economic and political crisis following 1965. For eighteen years he had led and guided the Egyptian revolution and had indelibly left his personal stamp on it. He was succeeded peacefully and without revolution by another of the Free Officers, Anwar al-Sadat; there is perhaps no better indication of Egypt's new character than this peaceful succession of governments.

Anwar al-Sadat is a very different man from Nasser. Where Nasser was flamboyant, quick, and daring, Sadat is circumspect, cautious, and deliberate. He does not have the charisma that Nasser had, and he is totally without the ability to hypnotize the masses or gain a great mass following. When he took office, many were disappointed and feared that he did not have the ability to rule Egypt and continue the revolution.

Yet Sadat has accomplished much. He has continued the pragmatic approach to economic and social change begun by Nasser. Rather than be swayed by ideology, he has done what he felt to be best for Egypt. He has therefore expanded the role of foreign and private investment in the economy, the trend Nasser had taken after 1967. Western companies have agreed to finance the pipeline joining the Red Sea with the Mediterranean. Negotiations with the American secretary of the treasury, William Simon, have resulted in an invitation to four American banks to open activity in Egypt. Sadat has not turned the tide of nationalization or socialism; he has simply reopened the country to capitalism and investment.

Under Sadat, foreign policy has likewise mellowed. New friendships have been established with the conservative and oil-rich Arab nations such as Kuwait and Saudi Arabia. Egypt no longer attacks the conservative Arabs as enemies of true Arab development; indeed, Kuwaiti and Arabian money now flows into Egypt to finance new industry, the army, and social improvements.

Sadat has swung Egypt away from the Soviet orbit and closer to a genuinely neutral stance. The Soviet advisers and technicians were asked to leave the country, and a coolness in Soviet-Egyptian relations has developed. Sadat attacked the communists as reluctant allies, who rarely gave Egypt all that she needed. A new friendship with the West has developed on the ruins of the Soviet friendship. The American President Richard Nixon visited Cairo in the summer of 1974 and promised the Egyptians that the United States would build nuclear reactors to provide electrical power for Egypt's expansion.

But the most dramatic success that Sadat has enjoyed was the Egyptian role in the Fourth Arab-Israeli War of October 1973. Neither side gained a decisive victory, but Egypt held her own against the Israeli army that had overwhelmingly defeated her in 1967. Most Arabs felt that their continual humiliation by Israel had come to an end; Sadat's reputation rose in the Arab World.

The oil boycott of the West followed, as a means to emphasize the united Arab demand that Europe and the United States change their policies in the Middle East. Radical Arab governments joined the traditional monarchies in emphasizing Arab solidarity, and an important element in this combination was Sadat himself, who, more than Nasser, was willing to work as an equal among the various leaders of the Arab World. The result has been a new settlement in the Middle East. The American secretary of state, Henry Kissinger, after strenuous weeks of diplomacy, worked out an agreement with Sadat and Assad of Syria that was also acceptable to Israel. Israel began to withdraw troops from occupied territory; President Sadat and other Arab leaders involved in the negotiations felt that the United States had shown new respect for the Arab cause. The peace was tenuous, but no one could doubt that a new balance of power had been introduced.

The Egyptian revolution under Nasser and Sadat has gone a long way toward breaking the vicious circle of poverty, ignorance, and general backwardness. Outstanding problems remain to be solved, but work has begun against some of the more distressing ones—disease, illiteracy, the degradation of women, and so on. It will take years to develop a strong economy comparable to the economies of better-developed countries, but the pragmatic approach of the government and the acceptance of both private and public sectors as essential promises well for the future if political stability can be maintained. The old feudal class is gone; estates have been broken up and land has been distributed. The working classes are better off. Many Egyptians now have a respect for government and an optimism for the future that their fathers did not have. Population still grows by leaps and bounds; there is still poverty, and the government has not solved unemployment. But who could expect the complete amelioration of a nation as backward as Egypt in two short decades? Isn't it enough that a beginning has been made?

CHAPTER SIX

The Second Revolution: Socialism in Algeria

The second revolution in the Arab World came in Algeria. This revolution presents a strong contrast with the revolution in Egypt. Algeria's relationship with her colonial master, France, had been far more intimate and intense than Egypt's had been with Great Britain, and France proved profoundly unwilling to shed her ties and power over her colony. Separation came only after a long, bloody war that devastated Algerian cities and countryside, raising the indignation of many throughout the world. Nasser's coup d'état had been painless and mercifully quick. Algeria's war was cruel and destructive. These two factors—the intimate colonialism between France and Algeria and the protracted War of Independence—determined Algerian Socialism and gave it its peculiar tradition and the traits that distinguish it from other forms of Arab Socialism.

After the eighteen-year war of pacification of Algeria was completed by France in 1848, thousands of Frenchmen and their families began to pour into the country, settling on land that had once been owned by Arabs and building cities that were rapidly to take on a French character. Immigration to Algeria became popular, and within a short time, a sizable portion of the Algerian population was European. By 1950 the descendants of the French settlers numbered one-tenth of the population, or nearly one million. In addition, many Algerians went to France to find work in factories and to form a source of low-wage labor for French industry.

The French in Algeria and their descendants held all the privileges that citizenship in France would have given them. They could vote, hold office, and rise in society. They set the style and fashion for the whole country, and thousands of Muslims chose to wear French clothing, speak French, and be educated in the French manner. Many gave up their faith, becoming nominal Christians, for no Muslim was permitted the same social and political rights granted Christians. The French believed in the superiority of their culture and tradition and felt almost a missionary's duty to raise the cultural level of the Algerians by making them into Frenchmen.

France brought many advantages to Algeria. Many Algerians were introduced for the first time to the modern world by French literature, science, and technology. France helped to turn Algerian eyes away from tradition and stagnation and toward the opportunities of the present day by spreading modern political and social ideas. France raised the level of Algerian agriculture and commerce. Modern agricultural techniques were introduced, irrigation systems built, and crop production improved. In the cities, new buildings arose and an expansion of crafts and small industries provided new jobs. Indeed, there was no rebellion against the French rule after 1871, and most felt that the two countries had settled down to peaceful association and amalgamation.

Yet the benefits brought by France were often overshadowed by the wrongs and evils. Improvements in Algerian agriculture and commerce had been made for the sake of France and of the French who had moved to Algeria. The impoverishment of the Arab population was often the natural outcome of French superiority. Old tribal systems were broken up and traditional institutions of authority and respect were discredited. Discrimination became common. Arabs were laborers and servants; no self-respecting French Algerian could allow himself to "sink" to the level of the Arab. Arabs found it difficult to buy land or to get jobs that offered more than the bare minimum for existence.

As the well-known psychologist of colonialism Frantz Fanon was to say in *The Wretched of the Earth*, Arab Algerians became convinced of their own inferiority and took on the mental attitudes of slaves. They lost faith in their own worth and believed that only the French knew how to govern and that only the French possessed a culture worthy of imitation and adoption. Working among Algerian Arabs in the 1950s, Fanon saw deep mental disturbances in many of the people he examined. These disturbances he attributed to colonialism and subjugation and noted that they often broke out in antisocial behavior such as criminality and impulsive violence. The cure, Fanon felt, would come only when the average Arab could express himself violently by rising up and overthrowing the colonial master.

The rise of Algerian nationalism has been noted in an earlier chapter. What brought these vague and relatively small movements to a head, however, and crystallized Algerian national sentiment generally, were a series of massacres that took place in Sétif and the Constantine region of Algeria in May 1945. In a burst of enthusiasm, many Algerians took to the streets on May 1 to celebrate an Allied victory over Germany that they felt was soon to happen. A single Algerian national flag was carried in the demonstration, and it was to this flag that the French officials reacted. Soldiers fired on the demonstrators, killing several Arabs. According to French figures, fifteen thousand Algerians were killed at Sétif in the rioting that followed (forty-five thousand according to reliable Arab sources). The rebellion expanded throughout the province, with the French reacting with special ferocity at Bône and Souk-Ahras. Algerians were shot and then buried in mass graves in lime pits.

Messali Hadj, the radical nationalist, reacted to the Sétif massacres by forming the Movement for the Triumph of Democratic Liberties (MTLD). The MTLD called for Algerians to begin a struggle for independence. It drew most of its support from the Muslim working class, students, and young intellectuals.

Between 1945 and 1948, the French toned down their repression and tyranny. Attempts were made to appease Algerian public opinion and placate the nationalist sentiment that had been aroused by the events at Sétif. Promises were made for free elections of delegates to a National Assembly that was to have substantial Muslim representation. But when the elections were finally held in April 1948, it could be proved beyond a shadow of a doubt that the French had rigged the outcome to prevent the election of Arabs. Likewise, the government arrested almost four hundred Muslims after the election, many of whom had run for office, but had admitted in their campaigns that they favored separation from France. Other elections in 1950 and

1951 were similarly rigged and did not have the confidence of the Arab population.

The failure of the elections of 1948 convinced several young Algerians that France would never relinquish her hold on Algeria and that armed resistance was called for. They broke away from Hadj's MTLD and formed the Organisation Spéciale (OS), the first secret organization of the revolution, and the group that was to initiate the War of Independence in 1954. The OS trained its members in the use of weapons and explosives and planned eventually to become a terrorist group. Hocine Ait Ahmed was the first leader of the OS, and among its early members was Mohammad Ben Bella. Both men were to be numbered among the "historic chiefs" of the Algerian Revolution. A post office in Oran was held up and $9,000 obtained for the organization's use. But in 1950 the secret police learned of the group and destroyed its stock of ammunition. Many of its members were sent to prison. Meanwhile, the Berbers, a people who speak a language unrelated to Arabic, had begun to carry on guerrilla war against the French in the mountain areas of western Algeria.

The police repression of the OS, however, did not put an end to revolutionary activity in Algeria. Many who escaped arrest fled to the remote areas of the country to await the coming revolution. Others fled abroad, to Paris, Cairo, Switzerland, and elsewhere, where they formed revolutionary groups in exile. By 1952 many were pressing for action.

The young men attracted to the early revolutionary movement were for the most part from modest and low-income Arab families. Ben Bella's family owned a small plot of land at Marnia that they worked and lived on. None came from families that had formed the traditional Arab elite and power structure before the coming of the French. Some were devout Muslims, such as Houari Boumedienne; others had lost their faith and had learned secularism and socialism from the French. What united them, of course, was a disgust with French rule and a belief that Algeria needed independence.

French authorities knew that some sort of clandestine revolutionary activity was taking place, but they did not consider it significant. It was thought that the French army in Algeria, numbering some seventy thousand, would be sufficient to meet any crisis. Besides, France was more preoccupied with Tunisia, where nationalist activity was stronger and more efficiently organized than in Algeria, and in Indo-China where a full-scale war was being waged against the French. The French had not counted on the dedication of the Algerian revolutionaries. In the spring of 1954, however, Algerian radicals had begun to set in motion the plans that would lead to rebellion. A date for the opening skirmish was decided upon, and the National Liberation Front—the central revolutionary party and organization—was born. Its aim, as it declared in its first public statement, was "national independence." The colonial system was to be liquidated and all corruption brought to an end. The revolution was to be guided by the principles of Islam, and the rights of all men, regardless of race or creed, were to be respected. In a statement of conciliation, the FLN, as the Front is commonly called, promised that bloodshed would be avoided as much as possible and that French interests would be respected. Negotiations were possible, it added, if the French entered them in good faith.

Algeria was divided into several revolutionary districts, with a trusted and able leader put in charge of all revolutionary activity in each. The insurrection began on November 1, 1954. At that time, the National Liberation Army (ALN) had only a few hundred members and very little in the way of weapons and ammunition. But once the revolution was under way, support began to pour in from many quarters. The Algerian working classes joined immediately. The FLN, which acted as the political and propaganda arm of the revolution, while the ALN was its muscle, spread word of the revolution's aims and solicited help or backing from wherever possible. Students were enthusiastic and organized strikes against the French in the larger cities, while many joined the ranks of the army and guerrilla bands.

Even the moderate nationalists, led by Ferhat Abbas, were converted. Throughout Algeria, devout and superstitious Muslims who had first ignored the rebellion soon came to praise the freedom fighters, often calling them "the companions of the Prophet returned to earth" and citing miracles the young revolutionaries had performed.

The early revolutionaries were not experienced politically. Their energy was largely exhausted in their effort to maintain and supply their army. They had only vague ideas of the organization and discipline required to win independence and establish a new government. But as the fighting continued, and Algerian losses were often severe, it became clear that some sort of overall plan was needed, a central revolutionary authority, that would guide the revolutionary movement as a whole. A secret congress was therefore held in the Soummam Valley in the summer of 1956 to discuss reorganization and renewal.

The Soummam Valley Congress created an executive committee of five, later enlarged to nine, members to oversee the revolution. These men were to supervise all activity, assure that there was little duplication of effort, and that available resources were to be used in the best way possible. They were likewise to see that the Algerian Revolution won support abroad, and that France was condemned for her colonialism.

The Congress issued several ideological statements that affected socialism as it later evolved in free Algeria. It condemned the "cult of the personality," whereby one charismatic revolutionary dictated all activity and reform. Instead, the Algerians opted for what they called a "college system," in which a committee of several men with different ideas sat down for discussions until they arrived at some policy they all could agree upon. Finally, the delegates at Soummam agreed that political considerations should always take precedence over military matters, and that Algerian independence would not result in military dictatorship.

Historians later called the early years of the war the "heroic years." The struggle of ill-equipped guerrilla bands against the large French force caught the imagination of people in many parts of the world. The French, who possessed the best weapons available, found it impossible to repress the Arabs who had the advantage of fighting on their own land for their own independence. Brutal and barbaric methods were often used to subjugate the Algerian nationalists. The French were not limited by humane considerations; thousands of Algerians were thrown into prison camps and tortured by French soldiers and police. The Algerians responded with acts of terrorism. French businesses, administrative buildings, and homes were bombed. The "Battle of Algiers" saw some of the most vicious and bloody fighting of the twentieth century. French paratroopers occupied the Muslim sections of the city and instituted a tyranny so harsh that it raised the protests of many world leaders.

As time passed, a new breed of revolutionary emerged. The early organizers of the FLN had been romantic revolutionaries. They were long on rhetoric and drama, deeply dedicated to the struggle for independence, but they had been short on a talent for administration and did not possess the ability to run a new government. The Soummam Valley Congress had tried to remedy this problem, but had not solved it completely. It was solved only gradually, as newer revolutionaries joined the ranks of the FLN. These newer revolutionaries were more deliberate, pragmatic, and practical than the older breed. They had been better educated, and their political consciousness was more sophisticated and modern. They knew that the revolution required expertise as well as dedication, and they were willing to act as ideologists, administrators, diplomats, or in any other roles for which technical ability and know-how was required. Among them was Colonel Houari Boumedienne, who soon became the able commander of all revolutionary forces and molded the army into an effective, well-trained unit.

The last years of the war were the most complex and bitter. Support came from many quarters. Senator John Kennedy, later President of the United States, spoke in the United States Congress on behalf of the revolutionaries. George Meany, an important American labor leader, urged the American workers to support the Algerian workers in their fight for freedom. Public opinion throughout the world was against the French. The Fourth French Republic collapsed for its failure to solve the Algerian crisis, and a Fifth Republic was established under the great World War II hero General Charles de Gaulle, who had long voiced sympathy for the Algerians. De Gaulle felt that France owed the Algerians a great deal for the support they had given France in the struggle against Nazism. He wanted to settle the Algerian war as quickly as possible.

Negotiations were begun with the revolutionary leaders. Arrangements were made for a French pullout and the establishment of Arab sovereignty over Algeria. In a last-ditch effort, however, the French Algerians arose against any settlement that would end French superiority. Several French generals mutinied against de Gaulle's orders, directing their soldiers to fight the Arabs and resist attempts to force the French out of Algeria. The campaign that these generals and the French Algerians waged against the Arab population was vicious and ugly. Schools and hospitals that had been built by French money for the Algerians were destroyed. Members of the rebellious army shot Muslims on sight in Algiers and elsewhere; they entered hospitals and murdered Muslims who were ill or wounded. Muslim teachers were executed before their pupils in the classrooms. The library of the University of Algiers was burned, and, on one occasion, a truck loaded with explosives was sent careering down a hill onto a dock where Algerian longshoremen were working, killing one hundred and twenty.

The idea behind this slaughter seems to have been the hope that the Muslims would declare a Holy War against the French, and that de Gaulle would be forced to change French policy and reenter the country to protect French life and property. But the plan did not work. The Muslims reacted to this violence and inhumanity with unusual patience and discipline. No wholesale reprisals or terrorist activities were carried out. Perhaps the Muslims could afford to be patient because they felt that peace was near. On May 19, 1962, a cease-fire was declared and the end came to Algeria's colonial status. Full celebration was scheduled for July 5, the anniversary of the French occupation of 1830.

The cost of the war had been stupendous. In a country of ten million, more than a million had died. Two million had been forced into regroupment camps within Algeria. Three hundred thousand were in exile in neighboring Arab countries, and one hundred and fifty thousand were in camps the French referred to as "Camps of Lodging," but which were really centers of psychological warfare and brainwashing. The economy was devasted by years of struggle and by the mass emigration of French technicians, landowners, and managers. French money was withdrawn from the country. Food was scarce because of poor harvests. Algeria had never been wealthy and prosperous, but the War of Independence exacerbated the poverty and backwardness the revolutionaries hoped to change.

The peace settlement with France brought little stability and order to Algeria. Even before the victory celebration the revolutionaries had begun to fight against one another. There had never been political agreement among them, and now when their common enemy had been defeated, a struggle for domination began, each group wanting to assume power in the new Algeria. Often these disputes were purely personal. Ben Bella and Mohammad Boudiaf, the original founder of the ALN, for instance, could not stand one another. Other disputes were more ideological—some feared the rise of a dictator; others wanted socialist reforms taken immediately. An assembly of Algerian revolutionaries met in Tripoli, Libya, and drew up a document that called for socialist transformation. The Tripoli Program, however, did not have the support of all Algerians.

The struggle became so fierce that many feared Algeria would break into full-scale civil war. Armies led by the leaders of different factions began to march on one another, but war was averted when the people of Algiers, in a dramatic, last-minute effort, placed themselves between two opposing groups of soldiers. Many in the crowd were women carrying their children; the feuding revolutionaries were shamed and forced to see that they were leading an already war-torn country into further war. The crowd in Algiers had shouted "we want bread; we don't want war" and "enough, seven years of war, enough." The factions agreed to settle differences and to allow the leader of one group, Mohammad Ben Bella, to assume control in the name of stability and order.

Ben Bella was forty-six when he became Algeria's head of state. He had been educated through secondary school, after which he joined the French Army. He served in the Italian campaign of World War II and was four times cited for bravery. After the war he joined Messali Hadj's Movement for the Triumph of Democratic Liberties but soon grew more radical. He was jailed for his work with the Organisation Spéciale but escaped and went abroad. He spent most of the War of Independence in French captivity. Later, Ben Bella would express regret that he had ever risen to power, but now he seemed the only revolutionary leader that most of the factions could agree upon. Even de Gaulle and Nasser hoped that Ben Bella would be chosen, for they had found him to be the easiest Algerian leader to deal with.

But from the beginning it became apparent that Ben Bella had chosen to rule arbitrarily. In order to secure his position, he dismissed any assistant or government administrator he grew suspicious of. Indeed, he replaced officials so often that Algerians joked their government had become the "waltz of the prefects." Chanderli, the man who had ably defended the Algerian revolutionary cause for many years in the United Nations, was rejected for no more reason than

Ben Bella considered him to be a "false militant." Other officials were played one against another to incite jealousies and prevent rival factions from growing too strong and seizing power.

When Ben Bella granted the nation a constitution, and an elected National Assembly sat to consider Algeria's problems, the delegates found themselves so intimidated and threatened by Ben Bella's men that few could express opinions of their own. And to assure political unanimity throughout the country, a secret police force was created to spy on dissidents and opposition movements. The press and radio were heavily censored; few literate Algerians could find out what was happening in their own country. Ben Bella invaded the judiciary, too, forcing judges to condemn his enemies and using them as tools of state. The right to strike was taken away from the labor unions, and labor leaders were threatened in the same manner as the National Assembly delegates and the judges.

The end result of this government by intimidation, force, and threat was a loss of respect for the achievement of independence and the revolutionary struggle. Many felt betrayed by the government. Yet Ben Bella's years in power were not entirely obsessed with power and repression. Education became a primary concern; indeed, the country devoted the largest part of its budget, after defense, to it. By 1965 the number of primary school students had doubled the figure before independence. The number of college students likewise increased, and assistance was given to students who wanted to study abroad. Serious efforts were begun to educate large numbers of teachers. In an effort to aid the large number of wartime orphans, Ben Bella instituted a program called "Operation Shoeshine Boys" to give work and income to this group that would have otherwise begged on the streets.

But to say that Ben Bella developed a coherent social and economic policy would be to stretch the truth. The Tripoli Program had given him a few general directives: the means of production would be nationalized; short- and long-term planning would be used to overcome Algeria's social ills. The character of the revolutionary government would be "national, revolutionary and scientific." The Tripoli Program also urged that the national leaders take care to establish close contact with the masses of people and consult with them in matters of state. Islam, it added, would guide all change.

These aims were vague, however, and there was much confusion and disagreement among the Algerian leaders who drafted them. Ben Bella did not feel confined by them. At one moment he would lend them support; at the next moment he would discard them and argue that Algeria needed another form of socialism. His closest advisers on socialist policy—the Algerian Mohammad Harbi and two foreign Marxists—had strong Trotskyite leanings, favoring an extreme communist movement that hoped to bring revolution to the whole world. All three tended to support a revolution that was far more radical and secular than the average Algerian would accept.

The result was hesitation and confusion. Socialist measures were announced that the government failed to carry into effect. The famous March Decrees of 1963 nationalized more than seven hundred thousand hectares (one hectare is equal to 2.471 acres) of land formerly owned by French Algerians. The decrees likewise seized and placed under Algerian management property—factories, businesses, and so on—that had been French controlled. But these socialist acts were not followed by any significant planning and administration. A totally haphazard and inadequate self-management program was instituted that resulted in drops in crop production and industrial output. Ben Bella boasted that Algerian workers and peasants now had control of their own land and factories but refused to recognize that this control was disastrous and threatening to ruin the country. Ben Bella nationalized many small concerns—cinemas, small factories employing under twelve people, and so on—the very sector that Nasser left in private hands; it seemed beyond Ben Bella's comprehension to see that these acts were not what Algeria needed.

The most lucid statement of Algeria's predicament during Ben Bella's government was the Charter of Algiers, drawn up in 1964 by Mohammad Harbi. It listed the grievances that plagued society and the economy: weak industry, underemployment, lack of technical personnel, continued dependence on France. It went on to elaborate a "socialist edifice" that would eliminate these grievances. But Ben Bella was never to act on the Charter and its proposals. Instead he relied on rhetoric to hide the failures of his administration. He compared the Algerian "agrarian revolution" to the Chinese and argued that socialism in Algeria was more successful than in Yugoslavia.

Ben Bella's foreign policy reflected the same dictatorial and misinformed qualities his political and social philosophy displayed. He had plans for an Algerian role in the economic recovery of South America and the liberation of Africa. He attempted to carry revolution into black Africa, but most of the black African leaders and revolutionaries came to denounce his aid as amateurish and unhelpful. He gained no reputation as a great Third World leader, and this was a source of major disappointment to him.

Hopes were high in Algeria after independence that some sort of unity could be established among the nations of the Maghrib—Morocco, Algeria, Tunisia. Each had recently secured its independence from France and each claimed the same Arab and Islamic traditions. Yet no agreement among the three nations was forthcoming. Habib Bourguiba, the Tunisian president, and Ben Bella quarreled repeatedly. Ben Bella thought that the Tunisians had proved traitors to the Arab cause by failing to join the FLN and its struggle in Algeria. The Tunisians had given aid and offered their country as a place of refuge for the Algerian army, but this was not enough for Ben Bella, who wanted the Tunisians to place themselves under the FLN. President Bourguiba never visited Algeria while Ben Bella was president, because of resentment over Algeria's attacks on Tunisian honor. The quarrel between the two nations came to a head in 1964, when Tunisia discovered oil within her territory, but near the Algerian border. Algeria immediately declared the oil her own and set out to discredit the boundaries.

But much more serious were Algeria's disputes with her neighbor on the other side, Morocco. Along that border, a large tract of land was in dispute. Morocco had given Algeria aid and support during the revolution, but relations between the two countries deteriorated rapidly until open warfare broke out in the late summer and early fall of 1963. Mohammad Harbi, Ben Bella's socialist adviser, hoped to exploit the conflict for the sake of socialism. He wanted to declare the war a struggle of revolutionary forces against the conservative, reactionary forces of the Moroccan monarchy. He likewise wanted to use the cause of war to mobilize the nation along socialist lines, nationalizing all property for the sake of the war effort. But again Ben Bella failed to take advantage of the situation. Instead, he saw the war along traditional nationalist lines, simply as a conflict between two countries for territory. Mobilization was haphazard and ill-planned; workers were taken from the fields and factories with no effort made to ensure continued production. The economy, already in a downward slump because of Ben Bella's mismanaged nationalizations of French land and property, fell even further. And to top it all off, the Moroccan army easily defeated the Algerian forces.

Ben Bella's relationship with the communist world was likewise uncertain and bewildering. The Algerian revolutionaries had taken a dim view of the communist movement from the beginning. The French Communist Party had at first failed to support the War for Independence, and the communist world as a whole had been slow in showing interest and support. In addition, many Algerians disliked Marxist philosophy, which they found incompatible with their ideas of Arab and Islamic tradition. In spite of this antipathy, however, Ben Bella did try to win support from the communist bloc and to obtain aid from the Soviet Union and China for the Algerian cause.

The communists proved willing to send military and economic aid, as well as groups of doctors and other specialists to help improve Algeria's standard of living. But the Algerians soon denounced the aid as insufficient and of low quality. Tractors sent from Yugoslavia were condemned because they did not compare well with American tractors. Soviet doctors were rejected because they were not as good and able as French doctors. The Algerians likewise resented the propaganda that came with every communist gift, feeling this propaganda to be an insult to Algerian independence. Finally, when additional aid from the communist world did not arrive to stem the growing economic crisis, Ben Bella was forced to realize that his relations with the communists had failed and that he must look elsewhere for help.

The only place he had to look, however, was to the old colonial master, France. The relation with France had never been completely severed after independence, in spite of the rhetorical and revolutionary claims of the Ben Bella government. Economic aid flowed from France, and the Algerian economy depended on it. More important, however, was the supply of trained personnel that came regularly from France. In 1964 nearly half the upper grades of the Algerian Civil Service were French. Fifteen thousand badly needed teachers were likewise French, and Ben Bella would have welcomed many more. French money also helped to pay compensation to former French Algerians who had lost their land and property.

What France wanted in return for this aid was the right to use the Sahara for her own purposes, and this she proceeded to do. On March 18, 1963, she exploded an atomic bomb at Ein-Ekker; many Algerians felt it to be a great insult. Here, an imperialist power was using Algeria to test weapons that might be used against socialist nations. Did the Algerians have no rights in their own nation? Public opinion also became incensed as it became clear that the Ben Bella government was extending benefits to private French firms to exploit the mineral wealth of the Sahara. Many felt that the government had not secured Algerian rights to these minerals—oil and natural gas— and was granting the European advantageous terms. Harbi warned that socialism could not be created in a nation where a foreign power held such a strong economic control, but Ben Bella was in a dilemma. His economy was rapidly collapsing, and he needed some assurance that money would continue to flow into the country to support his regime.

By the summer of 1964 open opposition to Ben Bella appeared throughout the country. Terrorist activity spread; many observers felt that a counterrevolution of considerable force was building. Within the government itself, opposition was centering around Houari Boumedienne, the head of the army. Boumedienne had consolidated his position in the years of independence and had gained many supporters, both civilian and military. In spite of efforts to isolate him or limit his power, he had emerged as the one source of effective resistance to Ben Bella.

Indeed, Boumedienne had grown to dislike Ben Bella's policies for some time. Ben Bella's tyranny was distasteful to him, and he had no stomach at all for Mohammad Harbi's doctrinaire socialism, which did not strike Boumedienne as nationalistic and religious. But Boumedienne bided his time and awaited the right moment to overthrow the government. That moment came in June 1965. In a wellplanned coup, he easily drove Ben Bella from power and began the second phase of the Algerian Revolution. Only four days earlier, the deposed ruler had claimed that his regime was more secure than ever.

The new government immediately began an attack to discredit Ben Bella and everything he had stood for. He was called ambitious and tyrannical, with little true feeling for Algeria or Islam. He was called vacillating and without a true concept of government. One close collaborator of Boumedienne's, Cherif Belkacem, pointed out that under Ben Bella Algeria had had many theories of socialism—Castro socialism, scientific socialism, and other kinds—but had experienced no true socialism. But greatest condemnation was reserved for Ben Bella's "cult of personality," which was called a betrayal of the aims of the revolution as expressed at the Soummam Valley Congress. Ben Bella had tried to make Algeria his own personal possession, and this had ended in disaster.

A proclamation set out the aims of the new government, revealing how different its goals were from those of the earlier regime.

> . . . the love of luxury must be replaced by integrity, improvisation by steady work, impulsive reactions by a state philosophy—in a word, realistic socialism based on the country's needs must replace day to day publicity seeking socialism.

To build this "truly socialist society," the proclamation argued, the government must take into account "our faith, our convictions, the secular traditions of our people and our moral values."

Boumedienne's revolution was the triumph of the younger, more educated revolutionaries who joined the FLN after the War of Independence had begun. They were more impressed with ability and efficiency than with rhetoric and display. Boumedienne's acts after taking office reveal the practical and more technically minded side of their thinking. The personal system of government was abolished, as were Ben Bella's constitution and the National Assembly. They were replaced by a twenty-six-member Council of the Revolution that reflected the military background of Boumedienne and most of his supporters. The first duty of the Council was to oversee the destruction of Ben Bella's highly centralized government structure and replace it with a system that emphasized local control and self-government. After 1965 the commune became the most important unit in Algerian government, with government control over the communes limited to the coordination of the ideas and programs begun in the various communes. The communes were comparable to the states of the United States, only smaller. Each commune had the right to initiate policy in various social and economic areas such as agriculture, industry, education, and the management of state property. Officers were to be elected to a communal assembly by universal suffrage. By resting government in a council of twenty-six, and by the creation of the communes, Boumedienne hoped to destroy all elements of Ben Bella's centralized government.

Soon after taking power, Boumedienne faced strong opposition from labor unions who felt that the government was not radical enough and from students with whom Ben Bella had been popular because of his education program. To meet this dissent, Boumedienne declared 1968 to be the "year of the party"—a period when emphasis would be placed on the FLN and its restructuring as the central political institution of the revolution. Boumedienne wanted the FLN to function in much the same manner as Nasser's Arab Socialist Union, as a force of political unity and education molding the nation together.

The social and economic policy of the new regime was slow to emerge, leading to attacks from the left that Boumedienne had betrayed the revolution. But since 1967 the expansion of government activity has been noticeable. Emphasis has been placed on heavy industry. The state has established chemical factories, steel and auto works, and has begun to manufacture tractors and diesel engines. Plastic and fertilizer factories are projected for the future. State-owned concerns now dominate in light industry, too, especially in textiles and other areas of agricultural produce.

Between 1967 and 1970, most European oil interests were nationalized, with the exception of Getty Oil, which had settled its differences with Algeria in 1968. Agreements more favorable to Algeria were negotiated with foreign companies exploiting the mineral wealth of the Sahara. The banks of Algeria had likewise been seized by the state. The dependence on France had been reduced; in 1961, 80 percent of Algerian trade had been with the mother country. By 1970, this was down to 45 percent.

The early '70s saw increased economic activity. An economic "Four-Year Plan" sought to increase the gross national product by government expenditure in many economic areas. Austerity measures introduced to assure a surplus in trade seemed to be working. Agreements with the United States on shipments of natural gas were reached, and this arrangement promised an important source of income for development.

The most disappointing area of transformation, however, was the "Agricultural Revolution." Large estates continued to be seized by the government, but the effort to distribute this land among the landless was slow and inefficient. Rural unemployment was high, and the future seemed to promise little to the large numbers of peasants. There was some attempt made to improve rural standards of living by building model villages to show the peasants what cleanliness and modern science could accomplish, but these villages had little effect.

Under Boumedienne, the expansion of education begun by Ben Bella has continued. In 1970, 55 percent of school-age children were in school. Plans are to extend education to all children by 1980. Arabization of education, the use of the Arab language in schools rather than French, has grown. In 1970 the first technical institute of agricultural was opened; a new university was established in 1970 at Oran.

In health and medicine the government has worked to make adequate care and services available to all. Doctors and other medical personnel must serve in state-run hospitals and clinics for a period of time in order to be licensed. Clinics providing free medical care and supervision have appeared throughout the country. Centers where medicine can be obtained have vastly increased in number and have been established in rural areas for the first time. To provide adequate and hygienic housing, the government has subsidized the building of new apartment complexes and other buildings, especially since 1969.

In foreign affairs, Boumedienne has proved more cautious than his predecessors. In 1972 he visited Morocco and Tunisia as part of a program to improve relations with those two countries. He slowly improved ties with the West, but stopped far short of embracing the West as an intimate ally. Indeed, Boumedienne has emerged as a sincere neutral leader in the Third World. In the fall of 1973 he hosted a meeting of the unaligned nations in Algiers and attacked both the United States and the Soviet Union as imperialistic giants exploiting and using the small nations for their own national interests. Indeed, his attack on Russia was, if anything, more severe than his attack on America. He continued Algeria's close association with France from necessity, but had slowly sought to remove Algeria's deep dependence on that country.

Under Boumedienne, Algerian socialism had been given direction and definite characteristics. It favored the exercise of authority by committee rather than by an individual. It favored local control and government over centralization. Like Egyptian socialism, it tended to be pragmatic rather than ideological, and to adapt to a given situation and crisis rather than risk total transformation of all social and economic structures. To many of the left, this was not true socialism: it was too cautious and time-serving. Yet it is difficult to imagine a system that would have maintained stability and order while undertaking change; the far left would probably have driven Algeria into civil war. Boumedienne's real achievement, then, has been to balance the various interests together that had broken out after independence and to have remained in power for the past nine years.

Has the vicious circle of poverty and backwardness been broken in Algeria? It is hard to tell. Enormous problems remain. The population still increases at far too great a rate for the economy to support. In a nation where between five hundred and eight hundred thousand remain out of work, seventy thousand new jobs a year are necessary just to meet the needs of those who grow old enough to work. The FLN, which Boumedienne hopes to revive and make the nation's one political party, remains apathetic and passive. Newspapers and other media are still censored by the government, and there is no freedom of expression.

Yet it would be wrong to say that the Algerian Revolution has failed. The new four-year plan of 1974–77 promises much in continued industrial growth and development. The stability brought by Boumedienne makes it possible that Algeria can develop peacefully and cautiously. With the improvements that have been made in medicine, education, and government administration, it is safe to say that Algeria has broken away from the cycle of backwardness and ignorance to a great extent, and that a better future is in store for her. In 1972, at the celebration of the tenth anniversary of victory over the French, Boumedienne announced that Algeria would so improve her standard of living by 1980 that she would no longer be a part of the Third World.

CHAPTER SEVEN

Arab Socialism in Syria and Iraq

Arab Socialism has found its most radical representatives in Syria and Iraq. Both nations have boasted of taking the most extreme social and economic measures in the Arab World; both have been virulent in their verbal attacks upon the West and upon Israel. Both countries likewise have instituted regimes that have been compared to Russia under Stalin or Germany under Hilter in their adoption of police state tactics and their suppression of dissent and individual liberty. This pattern has been especially true in Iraq, where a knock on the door in the middle of the night has often led to the execution or disappearance of those considered enemies of the regime in power.

The rigidity and intolerance of the Syrian and Iraqi governments are largely a reaction to the diverse ethnic and religious make-up of both nations. For in addition to the standard problems of all Arab countries—illiteracy, disease, overpopulation, and poverty—Syria and Iraq are plagued with sizable minorities that have traditionally fought with one another and refused to be forced into union with the others. Algeria has its Berbers and Egypt its Copts, but neither Egypt nor Algeria has experienced the problems of Syria and Iraq, where the tasks involved in unifying and creating a nation have proved difficult if not impossible.

In a country the size of South Dakota, with a population of six and a half million, Syria encompasses four distinct Islamic sects.

Most Syrians are Sunnite (Orthodox) Muslims, but there are sizable and vociferous communities of Druze, Alawite, and Ismaili believers who maintain their own customs and traditions. Even the Sunnite majority is divided racially between Arabs and Kurds, a nationless people more closely related to the Persians than to the Arabs. In addition, there are smaller groups of Christians, especially Greek Orthodox.

Iraq's complexion is even more varied than Syria's. The central plain of this country of nine million is inhabited by Sunnite Muslims, who have traditionally held most of the positions of power and prestige. Yet the Sunnites are in a minority even among the Muslim Arabs, for in the south of Iraq, a large number of Shiites are found. Shiism is an Islamic heresy that rejects much of the Sunnite tradition. The Iraqi Shiites are poor, less educated, and less developed than their more orthodox fellow countrymen, and they have often looked for support to Iran, a Muslim nation that has long been Shiite. In addition to this major division between the Arab Muslims, a third group makes the ethnic situation even more complicated. In the north are two million Kurds (almost a quarter of the total population) who form a fiercely independent group that has continually caused trouble for the ruling government. The tension created by this ethnic and religious division has been exacerbated by social and economic backwardness and has made the vicious circle of poverty and human misery all the more onerous.

The diverse and warring minorities of the two countries have often seen their differences reflected in modern history. Since World War II, Syria and Iraq have endured a series of revolutions and coups that have given the Middle East a reputation for instability and disorder. There have been at least eleven changes of government in Syria alone. Since 1950 Iraq has experienced five or more (depending on the method of reckoning), but the changes in Iraq have been far bloodier and more violent than those in Syria. Revolution in Iraq has gained a reputation for bloodthirstiness and extremism.

The first revolutionary coup d'état came to Syria following the Arab-Israeli War of 1948. The Arab defeat disillusioned many Syrians with their government, which was a coalition of tribal chieftains, wealthy merchants, and other notables attempting to hold together a country in disorder after the departure of the former French masters. The failure of the Arabs in the war was blamed on the incompetence of the rulers and a great demand arose for immediate change. In 1949 Brigadier General Husni Zaim became Syria's first dictator. He sought advice from Michael Aflaq, one of the founders of the Baath, or Arab Renaissance Party, a movement that was gaining popularity throughout the Arab World.

But Aflaq and Zaim soon quarreled over ideological matters. Aflaq was imprisoned, tortured, and forced to sign a statement supporting the regime before he was released. Then he fled to Brazil. Three more coups followed in the next two years. All were carried out by army officers who could not be considered radical or socialist, but at the same time socialist sentiment was growing. Among young army officers and students, and among the minorities such as the Alawites and the Druze, Aflaq's socialism was popular. A second socialist group, founded by Akram al-Hourani, called the Arab Socialist Union, was likewise important. Opposing the two leftist parties was the Syrian Socialist Nationalist Party, a fascist group that spoke of a Syrian Empire that included much of the Middle East and the island of Cyprus.

Another coup d'état in February 1954 placed Colonel Feisal al-Atasi in power. Al-Atasi crushed the Socialist Nationalist Party, which had opposed him violently, and the Baath Party emerged as the most influential and significant ideology among the army officers. But the Baathists did not consider themselves strong enough to rule and remained in the background. They were concerned about the quick turnover of Syrian governments and did not want to assume power themselves until things became more stable and secure.

Meanwhile, Nasser had taken power in Egypt and was gaining respect and admiration throughout the Arab World. Many Syrians were coming to believe that Syria's future lay with Egypt in a united Arab state that could confront the world with Arab determination and strength. Many Syrians were likewise concerned about the power of Bakdash's Syrian Communist Party, which had gained influence because of the weakness of the other parties. In 1957 Aflaq, who had returned from South America, and Salah Bitar, his friend and co-founder of the Baath Party, went to Nasser and asked him to join Syria with Egypt. There was great fear that the Syrian communists— by far the strongest Communist Party in the Middle East—would

nomic reforms. In 1964 the Sixth Congress of the Baath Party announced the aims for the transformation of Syrian society. The party chose "Unity, Freedom and Socialism" as its slogan. The Baathists claimed they were bringing the "spirit of modern times to the Arab National Movement . . . by linking the nationalist revolution with the socialist revolution." In opposition to Egypt, the Syrians announced that they were opposed to one-man rule and in favor of collective leadership. Workers and peasants were given the right to criticize party activity. Syria would become a thoroughgoing democracy where all classes, races, and religious groups had equal freedom and the right to participate. Two years later another statement of party policy articulated more clearly the goals of the Baath. These goals and desires were

> . . . to create Arab unity, develop Arab economy on the basis of socialism and to free the Arab nation from all external and internal factors which may adversely affect national sovereignty or human freedom. The revolutionary regime strives to make all its policies serve a humanistic end which is to support national liberation movements and to cooperate sincerely with all countries for this purpose.

The Baath government has not rested on party platforms and rhetoric. It has put much of its radicalism into practice, and to a greater extent than neighboring Iraq, also a Baathist-run nation, the Syrians have created a socialist state. In 1963, after overthrowing the rightists, the Baath began to restore the socialist measures that had been undertaken during the period of union with Egypt. The government renewed agrarian reform and seized the large estates. The amount of land a man could own was severely limited, but this amount varied between populated, fertile regions, and isolated, arid regions of the country. Banks and main industries were nationalized. In 1964 and 1965 the government confiscated virtually all businesses that employed more than twelve people. One of the most significant accomplishments was the building of the Euphrates Dam, a dam that added large tracts of land to cultivation and provided a great source of energy. The port cities of the Mediterranean were developed, as was the transportation system of the country as a whole.

A great deal of effort was expended on indoctrination and propaganda. All members of the Baath Party had to work in the fields with the peasants at harvest time; here they were to talk with the peasants, win their friendship, and explain the socialist revolution to them. Baathists also took jobs in factories and industries to help indoctrinate Syrian workers. The government has also directed concerted effort toward education and health care, but in both areas Syria has much work to do. The country cannot possibly train the number of scientists, doctors, and other technicians that it needs to run a modern socialist economy and society. Almost three-fourths of Syrian university students study subjects such as language, history, law, or art; as a result, many find it difficult to get a job related to their education and training.

The government has given important consideration to the army. It has been expanded and modernized, outfitted with weapons from the Soviet Union and other communist countries. Military service is compulsory for all males over eighteen. Service lasts for two and a half years, and the state has seen to it that the training program includes technical and general, as well as the expected military, instruction. The army is responsible not only for defense of the country; soldiers also work on road construction, public health projects, and other public services. A more pernicious duty of the army is to oversee the mass media and control newspapers, television, and radio. Freedom of expression is not allowed, and enemies of the state often find themselves imprisoned or exiled.

In foreign affairs, Syria has several times, since the Baathist coup, attempted to play an aggressive role in the Middle East. After being soundly defeated in the Arab-Israeli War of 1967, the Syrians gave equipment and aid to Palestinian guerrillas operating in Lebanon in 1969. In September of the next year, two hundred and fifty tanks were sent into Jordan to aid rebels fighting King Hussein, and in May 1973 Syria allowed Palestinian guerrillas to use Syria as a base for raids against Lebanon.

But since Major General Assad took power in the bloodless coup of November 15, 1970, he has curtailed these acts of aggression against conservative Arab states. Indeed, the rashness of his predecessor, Salah Jadid, who had precipitated an international crisis by sending tanks against Hussein, had driven Assad to seize power. In many ways, Assad has been the best thing that has happened to Syria for some time. He has never been an overly ambitious man, preferring to work on the sidelines and let others take the credit. He could have been the Syrian national leader long before he chose to be, but waited until crisis made his rise to power necessary.

Since the end of 1970, Assad has altered the complexion of Syrian socialism. He has chosen to speak directly to the people of the country over radio and television, giving them a sense of government participation they had not experienced before. This style is directly opposed to that of his predecessors who preferred to remain faceless and impersonal, running the country quietly while the masses of people went along with little knowledge of their government and its leaders. Assad has likewise toned down surveillance by the secret police and has made it easier for foreigners to travel in Syria without being molested.

Assad has made attempts to end the corruption in government administration. Several officials have been brought to trial for abuse of authority and excessive use of violence against prisoners. Although the government still controls the most important sections of Syria's economy—the large electricity plants, the railroad, the oil refineries, and so on—Assad has encouraged a revival of private business in the hopes of establishing a vital private sector in the economy. Foreign investment from the West is now encouraged, and the government is trying to lure wealthy middle-class Syrians who fled the country back to Syria to help raise the standard of living and create a healthier economy.

In foreign affairs, Assad has likewise helped to mellow the former Syrian intransigence. He has made moves to settle disputes between King Hussein and the Palestinian guerrillas. In an amazing turn-about, he no longer allows the Syrian state-owned radio to attack and vilify conservative Arab leaders such as the late King Faisal of Saudi Arabia. Before Faisal's assassination, he and Assad settled many differences and established a relationship between their two countries that bodes well for stability in the Middle East.

In the summer of 1974 Assad even began negotiations on the Israeli problem—Syria in the past had adamantly opposed any settlement with Israel—and welcomed the American secretary of state, Henry Kissinger, to Damascus. The American President, Richard Nixon, likewise visited the Syrian capital, the first American President to do so while in office. These events had seemed impossible only six months earlier; clearly a new day had dawned in the Middle East.

But no one can say with assurance that Assad will remain in power. Recent history has shown that no Syrian regime is stable, and only time will tell if the new Syrian leader will follow the fate of many others. So many problems remain to be solved that stability seems the one thing Syria needs most of all. Large numbers of men and nearly all women are unemployed. Population is growing by leaps and bounds. Housing is a severe problem, for large numbers of people are leaving the countryside to find work in the cities. Fifty percent of the nation still cannot read or write. Many Syrians who are professionals—doctors, engineers, and others—leave the country to find work elsewhere; there is a drain on what trained personnel the country has. Defense expenditure has placed a severe bind on the economy, so that many public projects have been abandoned or neglected. The vicious circle is clearly still at work in Syria, but many optimists feel that it can be broken if Assad's government is permitted to carry its program into effect.

Iraq has been more fortunate than the other radical Arab lands. It possesses enough cultivatable land to feed its population, and it is blessed with an oil supply that scientists believe comprises at least 6 percent of the world's known reserves. Indeed, many observers agree that Iraq has been well treated by nature and could solve many of its social and economic problems long before the less endowed Arab countries, such as Syria and Egypt, may be able to do so.

But if Iraq has been fortunate in its natural resources, it has been disastrously unfortunate in its politics and history. Division and civil war are common. In the summer of 1974 the sixteen-year-old Kurdish-Iraqi War flared up again and the Iraqi army marched north to pacify the Kurds. However, by the spring of 1975 the Kurds faced total defeat. Iran, their principal ally, unexpectedly withdrew its support—as part of budding friendly relations with the Iraqi government. The resolution of differences, including a long-standing border dispute, between the two countries would greatly enhance the possibility of lasting peace in the region.

Revolution first came to Iraq in 1958. For two decades, Iraq had been controlled by a strong man, Nuri al-Said. All political parties had been outlawed; some, such as the communists, faced harsh repression and the execution of many leaders. The government seemed to be run for the benefit of the large landowners, the wealthy merchants, and the tribal chieftains. The corrupt monarchy held the respect of no one. Nuri al-Said was a friend of Great Britain, and allied Iraq with British causes and interests. In the '50s he negotiated a treaty, called the Baghdad Pact, whereby Iraq joined the English and other nations in a ring of defense around the Soviet Union.

In doing so, however, Nuri al-Said aroused the anger and enmity of Colonel Nasser in Egypt. Nasser was popular in Iraq and throughout the Arab World, a fact that made al-Said intensely jealous. Nasser attacked the old dictator sharply for his intimacy with the British; he warned Iraq that a new day had dawned in the Middle East, and no longer would European interests be allowed to take precedence over Arab interests. A sizable number of young officers in the Iraqi army likewise began to oppose their government and to organize a Free Officers movement modeled on Nasser's in Egypt. The young officers, who formed several revolutionary cells in the army, contacted civilian leaders sympathetic to reform, but the real leadership remained with the officers. Abdul Karem Kassem, the highest ranking officer among the conspirators, was chosen leader.

On July 14, 1958, Brigadier General Kassem and his followers seized Baghdad and proclaimed a republic. The king was deposed; he and the crown prince were murdered. Soldiers took the capital's radio station and occupied the principal government buildings. Nuri al-Said at first escaped but was later found and put to death. Most people received the end of the monarchy and dictatorship with relief. Support for Kassem and the revolutionaries was widespread. The new government released political prisoners and invited back to Iraq all people who had fled the terror of the old regime. Outlawed political parties were allowed to function in the open. A provisional constitution declared that the revolutionary government would work for the creation of a new society with equal rights for all citizens.

The government launched social and economic reform programs. Agricultural reform began with a five-year plan under which the amount of land a man could own was limited to five hundred acres of nonirrigated or two hundred and fifty irrigated acres. Land was distributed to the peasants. The government proceeded to nationalize basic industries and to plan for industrial expansion. A loan was obtained from the Soviet Union to finance new industry and other projects. After two years of rule, Kassem revealed a broad blueprint for the development and modernization of Iraq, and he began to arrange for further loans to finance this blueprint. The year 1961 saw the establishment of more than one hundred and fifty new industries and agricultural-related factories. By then, Kassem had broken up and distributed more than 60 percent of the arable land obtained from the seizure of large estates.

But Kassem's rule, however revolutionary, had proved unpalatable to many. A large number resented his one-man tyranny, where all change and reform underwent his personal scrutiny and approval. A statement released by the government while Kassem was still at its head revealed the degree of his dictatorship. In it, he was given superhuman revolutionary skills and power:

> The personality of the leader of the Revolution appeared closely linked with all events. Despite his modesty and his refusal to indicate, even indirectly, that he is the sole leader, organizer, and planner of the Revolution, people immediately discovered that Abdul Karem Kassem possessed unique characteristics, and a deep understanding of history and contemporary international policy and that he was a skillful organizer of extensive reform plans.

During his five years of rule, Kassem managed to alienate almost every segment of Iraqi political thought and influence. He quarreled with fellow officers who had joined him in his revolt against the old order. He lost the support of Iraqi nationalists, and he was distrusted by the Iraqi communists even though the Soviet Union was his chief ally. The Kurds, whom he tried to placate, arose against him. Kassem tried to eliminate opposition by imprisonment and execution; he played one faction against another, nationalist against communist, Kurd against Arab. His chief support remained the army.

But even that support eroded. Kassem's plans for a union with Syria fell when the United Arab Republic was announced, and Kassem, try as hard as he might, could never capture the leadership of the Arab revolutionary movement from Nasser. Plans to incorporate the oil-rich sheikhdom of Kuwait into Iraq likewise failed, as did Kassem's negotiations with oil companies to give Iraq a larger share of stock and revenue. With so many failures, there was little reason to keep him in power, and it came as a surprise to no one that Kassem was overthrown in February 1963 and quickly put to death.

The men who overthrew Kassem were army officers, members of

the Baath Party. They asked Abd as-Salem Arif to become president of the new government; Arif was one of those who had quarreled with Kassem and had broken with the former leader. He was a respected officer and nationalist. The office of premier was given to Colonel Ahmed Hassan al-Bakr, who was to play a prominent role in Iraqi politics several years later. A National Council for Revolutionary Command was set up and was composed of military as well as civilian leaders.

But the Baath government introduced no new revolutionary principles into Iraqi life. Its chief effort was to attack and discredit Kassem; the National Guard was given permission to repress communists by imprisoning and executing them. This the National Guard did with a vengeance and gained a reputation for extremism and torture. Soon Baathists were quarreling with themselves over policy. Some wanted to take immediate, radical measures to transform society; others, perhaps the majority of the party, wanted to change things slowly and provide the economic basis they felt necessary for the establishment of socialism. But perhaps the chief shortcoming of the Baathists was their inexperience in governing; many were very young and just out of school, where they had joined the party during years of youthful idealism and radicalism. They had little knowledge of administration and little familiarity with the very real problems that Iraq faced.

Thus, in November 1963, only nine months after assuming power, the Baath leaders were placed under arrest, and President Arif, who had been the highest non-Baathist in the government, assumed full power. Arif proved capable of giving the government direction, which it had not had under the Baath Party, and was supported by the army. He slowly set about to consolidate what gains had been made under Kassem and to give the country stability. On the first anniversary of his rule, he made a speech outlining the aims of his government. Its general goals, he said, were equality and social justice. He attacked the Baath for their mismanagement of the country and said that, above all, Iraq needed to develop economic self-sufficiency. He asked for war against Israel and promised that his regime would remain true to Islamic law and tradition. He went on to describe the intimate relation his government had with the military:

The government is proud to have originated from among

the Armed Forces and shall continue to equip and organize these forces with the latest weapons. Our army shall remain aloof from all party activity and politics and shall be this country's great pillar of strength.

In May 1964 Arif began to carry out his hopes for social justice and equality by the promulgation of a new constitution that adopted socialism. In July the government nationalized the banks, insurance companies, and several industrial and commercial enterprises. Steps were taken to create a Socialist Union, on the order of Nasser's Arab Socialist Union, that would educate the Iraqi in the goals and ideas of socialism and that would eventually bind the diverse nation together. Within a year, the government had confiscated more than half of the foreign-owned commerce and three-quarters of the manufacturing enterprises.

But by September 1965 Arif had become convinced that many of his socialist measures were far too radical and ill-conceived and that they brought no social justice but only economic disruption. He invited a prominent civilian lawyer, Abd ar-Rahman al-Bazzaz, to form a new government that would bring economic order. Al-Bazzaz agreed to take power, promising to preserve the socialist measures but increase the vigor and strength of the economy as a whole. Al-Bazzaz likewise planned to eventually establish a permanent democratic government, with regular elections and a parliament.

But fate intervened and brought an end to what might have been the first genuinely civilian radical government in the Arab World. Arif died accidentally in a helicopter crash in the spring of 1966. His older brother, Abd ar-Rahman Arif, was chosen by the army to replace him. But the military also put pressure on the older Arif to dismiss Bazzaz, who had incurred their displeasure because of his attempts to create a civilian government. Abd ar-Rahman Arif ruled with the army's help until July 1968, when the right wing of the Baathist Party seized power and drove Arif and his supporting officers from power. Ahmad Hassan al-Bakr, who had been in the government during the short-lived Baath regime of 1963, became president.

The Baath, with some shifts in leadership and party policy, have managed to remain in power. By 1970 the real power behind Bakr was Sadda Hussein al-Takriti, the deputy chairman of the Revolutionary Command Council, but al-Takriti preferred to remain in the background and rule through a figurehead. Socialism continued to make headway. State planning became an integral part of the country's transformation into a modern, industrial state. Iraq was most fortunate in its oil revenues, which provided a large income and made possible many of the socialist schemes for improvement and reform. Significant improvement has been made in education, and today nearly 70 percent of Iraqi boys are enrolled in schools, as are about 35 percent of the girls. The state has boasted that by the early 1980s, all school-age boys and girls will be in school, that illiteracy will be wiped out, and that Iraqis will be prepared with the modern industrial training and skills they need.

Health and welfare services have also improved, but remain behind the services provided in Syria, Egypt, and Algeria. The countryside remains largely unaffected by these improvements, but in the larger cities, and particularly in Baghdad, housing programs for the poor and the expansion of other welfare projects have made some inroads into the age-old problems of poverty and disease.

In foreign affairs observers have noted a major shift of Iraqi interests in the past two years. Earlier, Iraq had faced west, and had joined in the wars against Israel. Now, however, Iraq has turned her eyes, for the first time since the era of Kassem, toward Kuwait, the oil-rich sheikhdom to the south. Tension has increased between the two countries, and border violations have been reported. Since so much of Iraq's future depends on her own oil reserves, she sees Kuwait, which has 15 percent of the world's reserves, as a prize worth fighting for.

Iraq seems to be resolving its conflict with Iran. Both countries want to control the Persian Gulf, where so much of the world's oil begins its trip to the West. Control of the gulf would give Iraq power in the Middle East she does not now possess. The long border between Iraq and Iran is also a cause of contention; a brief war flared up in the spring of 1974, as both countries claimed the other had violated its territory. Iraq also carries on a squabble with its other neighbor, Syria; in spite of similar interests, neither country can come to terms with the other, the most recent conflict having arisen over the rate of revenue Syria charges for the transportation of Iraqi oil by pipeline to the Mediterranean seaports.

Yet the most important continuing problem that Iraq has to face is the Kurdish Question. In 1970 the Baathists promised the Kurds that many of their grievances would be eliminated; there would be aid to revive the Kurdish educational system, Kurds would be proportionally represented throughout all levels of the government, and Kurds would be placed in high government positions. The Kurds, however, soon grew suspicious of these promises when the government failed seriously to implement them. Fighting broke out again, and by the summer of 1974 Kurdish guerrilla bands were at war with the two battalions of the Iraqi army that had occupied the Kurdish section of the nation. Fighting was often intense and bitter, but in March of 1975, Iran, after agreements negotiated in Algiers, ceased to arm and support the Kurds. Under their admired leader, Mulla Mustafa al-Barzani, the Kurds vowed to fight on against overwhelming odds; the future promised little more than severe repression and futile rebellion.

It is easy to be critical of the Baathist governments of Syria and Iraq. Both countries have been bywords for political instability and chaos, and many political scientists pass over them as politically immature and hopeless. Yet such comments are not entirely fair. It is hard to imagine any party or group that could have come forward to run the countries and establish the needed order and stability. Any party that rose to power would probably have relied on tyranny, violence, and denial of freedom to remain in power. Where would the peaceful, democratic forces have come from? Genuinely respected and responsible government may not yet be a reality in Syria and Iraq, but the shortcomings must be balanced against the successes: some degree of equilibrium has been achieved, and progress has been made in education and public welfare. Many Syrians and Iraqi have been introduced to the modern world, and a few have become politically aware. One can only hope that in the crucible of present-day Syria and Iraq, a better future is being molded.

CHAPTER EIGHT

Conclusion

Arab Socialism has been the most articulate and dramatic expression
to date of the awakening that began in the Arab World more than a
century ago. That awakening arose in reaction to a political and social
crisis of sobering proportions; Arab poverty, ignorance, and misery
became obvious to anyone with open eyes and a mind unclouded by
tradition. Thoughtful Arabs set about looking for solutions to the
crisis. From the writings of al-Afghani, who looked for revival through
a religious renaissance, to those of Michael Aflaq, who created the first
coherent body of Arab Socialist thought, there has been a clear line
of development. All have looked for some answer to the political
apathy, indifference, and fear of government derived from centuries
of misrule and government irresponsibility. The search has not been
easy.

In addition, the political and social activists have grown more
aware over the past century of the needs and desires of the Arab
World. The revolt led by Colonel Urabi in 1881 against British presence in Egypt foreshadowed the full-scale nationalist movements of
the twentieth century. The nationalists sought the means and methods to make the Arab nations strong and independent; they tried
Western-style democracy, fascism, and other ideologies before settling, in the four countries discussed here, on several varieties of Arab
Socialism. History has not been kind to these nations—upheaval, civil
war, and disorder have long been part of their inheritance. But the

doctrines and practice of Arab Socialism have gone a long way toward answering the nationalists' hopes for strength and respectability.

Arab Socialism, therefore, is an ideology developed in response to the social and economic crisis in the Middle East, as well as to the fact of political backwardness and weakness. Arab Socialism has an advantage because its nationalism is beyond question, but at the same time it goes beyond simple nationalism by offering a range of radical social reform offered by no other Arab movement of comparable nationalist fervor. The popularity of Arab Socialism has arisen from its offering of radical solutions outside the context of a secular, anti-nationalistic Marxism. In nations where independence and self-determination were prime goals, Marxism and communism smacked of submission to the Soviet Union; a third way, outside of East or West, had to be found.

In the twenty-one years that have elapsed since the Free Officers seized power in Egypt, it is easy to discern a general pattern and characteristics common to the revolutionary governments in the Middle East and North Africa. In each country it has been the military that has instigated and undertaken the revolution. This is understandable. The military provides a means for education and advancement for young middle-class and lower-middle-class Arabs who could have found upward mobility otherwise difficult or impossible. In their training, these young men were made aware, as no others in their countries, of the weakness and backwardness of the Arab World. As young officers they formed a natural elite, the only disciplined elite, that could lead their nations to independence and modernization.

When the young men seized power in the name of nationalism and social justice in Egypt, Algeria, Syria, and Iraq, they discovered that the ability to govern was far more difficult than they had thought. They were naïve and inexperienced, and when their idealism was faced with the day-to-day tasks of government, they often found they had to sacrifice their original principles. Nasser abandoned hopes for freedom of speech in Egypt when it became apparent that many factions were dedicated to his overthrow. In each country strong men emerged from the ranks of the officers to give order and stability to the revolution. In Egypt this strong man was accepted and praised by the majority; in Syria, Iraq, and Algeria, the era of the strong man was followed by a period of rule by committee in which the "cult of personality" was condemned as unrevolutionary. Even Egypt, after Nasser's death, retreated from the idea of the charismatic leader.

The early months and years of the revolution were the most radical and extreme. Leftist rhetoric was blustering and unrelenting; it was claimed that all past wrongs and injustices were being swept away and a new order was being created. In Egypt this period lasted for a decade and a half; in Algeria it ended in three years with the fall of Ben Bella. In Syria and Iraq it has been active until recently. But in each radical Arab land, an era of mellowing and quieter deliberation followed the violent, arrogant years. Egypt was toned down in the last years of Nasser's rule and under Sadat. Algeria has been cautious and careful under Boumedienne. Even Syria, under Assad, seems destined to become more calm and collected. Only Iraq still resorts, from time to time, to its older, unrelenting rhetoric and leftism, but even Iraq has become quieter in its attacks upon Israel. This pattern follows the general revolutionary pattern recorded by historians of revolution; America, France, and Russia likewise experienced periods of rule under strong men—Washington, Napoleon, Stalin—who consolidated revolutionary gains and gave stability and direction to their nations. These nations also saw a toning down of revolutionary sentiment and dedication as time passed and men became more mellow. If the Middle East continues to follow this model, it can look forward to years of hard work and progress under its new system.

Has Arab Socialism worked in the countries where it has taken hold? In order to be fair, the critic of Arab Socialism, whether in Egypt, Iraq, Algeria, or Syria, must judge its achievements by what had been set up as goals. It would be ludicrous and unfair to judge the Arab World by the standards of Europe or America, where centuries of development have formed modern, progressive nations. The general goals of Arab Socialism have been the end of colonialism and imperialism, the destruction of feudalism, the attainment of pride and dignity, and the establishment of social justice. A more remote goal was the achievement of unity among the Arab nations, a unity that would transcend the petty squabblings of the various tribes and states and unite, for the first time since the tenth century, the lands that make up the Arab World.

It must be admitted that many of the goals have been attained.

The colonial powers have been driven from Algeria, Egypt, Syria, and Iraq, often after long periods of struggle. Imperialism and exploitation by Western economic interests have likewise been largely erased. Twenty-five years ago these nations could look forward to futures tied closely to Western business and enterprise, futures that would have kept the wealth in the hands of the few and would have maintained social and economic conditions as they had been for centuries. Now, in large part the result of radical governments, each country has attained some sort of self-sufficiency.

Feudalism has ended, and the various Arab radical regimes have made serious efforts at eliminating the privileged class with all its corruption and idleness. Twenty-five years ago, an Egyptian aristocrat might refuse to do any work, even refuse to carry his own briefcase. He might own an enormous estate worked by peasants whose economic situation had not changed for a millennium. He would feel no responsibility to improve the condition of thousands of his countrymen who slaved and starved. Now, the enormous estates have come to an end, and efforts have been made to distribute land to the landless.

Corruption too has been largely eliminated. Bribe and payoff had been part of Arab government for decades, part of the system that had condemned the Arab World to poverty and backwardness. The Arab World had been synonymous with corruption on a large scale; now, although corruption has not entirely disappeared, it has been severely curtailed, and more government officials work for the betterment of the country as a whole rather than for the benefit of their own bank accounts. Perhaps not all government administrators are as honest and austere as a Nasser or a Boumedienne, but none can be accused of the lavishness and extravagance of a King Farouk. This public discipline has been no mean achievement.

Arab Socialist regimes have also worked hard to attain goals of social justice. They have not attained their goals—no society establishes social justice in so short a time, if ever at all—but they have taken broad steps to improve the condition of workers and to expand hospital and health facilities. A shortage of trained personnel helps prevent rapid transition to a more modern and efficient society, but programs of health insurance, disease eradication, and old-age care have transformed the standards of living of many in the Middle East.

In all Arab countries that have adopted radicalism, the role of women has been expanded and many women have found new freedom and opportunity, if not liberation. Years will pass before the whole of society accepts this new freedom, but a beginning has been made. Education facilities are now available to far more than before independence, and in Egypt alone illiteracy is down from 77 percent to 50 percent.

But perhaps the most noticeable and remarkable achievement has been the development of Arab pride and self-esteem. Europeans had noted for centuries the complacency of the Arab World, a complacency that condemned the Arabs to backwardness and ignorance. There was a feeling among the Arabs that greatness lay in the past and could no longer be achieved. The West had permanently eclipsed the Arabs, it was felt, and all the Middle East had to look forward to was more of the same: economic stagnation, colonialism, and poverty.

In a few short years radical Arab leaders and governments have gone a long way toward dissolving that feeling and moving toward the creation of a new attitude: one that sees government capable of improvement, one that is willing to attack social problems, and one that is willing to commit itself to long-term goals such as social justice. Fatalism and quietism have begun to disappear from the Arab consciousness. Perhaps this is the real and lasting revolution in the Arab World, a change of mind and attitude from traditional, conservative ways to patterns that welcome transition and change. In this, the radical regimes have led the way and have contributed to growing Arab pride.

But just as it is the duty of the critic to point out those areas where Arab Socialism has been successful, so it is his duty to show where these governments have often fallen far short of their goals, and, on occasion, have betrayed them. For instance, it is clear that the former colonial powers have been driven from the Middle East, and that American or European corporations no longer exploit the rich oil and mineral supplies without due compensation. But it is equally clear that the radical regimes have overreacted in their hatred of the West and its power. Soviet influence has increased; Syria, and especially Iraq, today boast of intimate relationships with the communist world. Egypt and Algeria have been more circumspect, and

Egypt even ejected many Soviet advisers and military personnel. The fact remains, however, that many radical governments drove one kind of foreigner from their shores, only to welcome another. Where the Soviets have invested large sums of money, they are not likely to remain objective and disinterested. Just as Western capitalists are concerned about their investments, so the Russians want returns on their arms and money. The Arabs have substituted one form of obligation for another.

Next, the development of self-esteem and pride is not entirely a beneficial and welcome achievement. In the full growth of their national awakening, the Arabs have shown a pride and patriotism that destroys their sense of reality and distorts the true measure of their achievement. In their struggle with Israel, the Arabs at times seem to have forgotten that defeat of the Jews will not bring an answer to the problems that face the Middle East. The last Israeli could be driven into the sea, but illiteracy, poverty, a high birthrate, and the other severe problems would still exist and need to be solved.

The Arab socialist nations must likewise be criticized because they have often abandoned and forsaken the democratic goals they set for themselves. This is not a simple case of failing to attain difficult ideals; it is rather a case where these goals were forgotten or put aside, where expediency and efficiency were allowed to do away with civil and individual freedom. It is a common characteristic of Arab radical governments that they are run by military men or by former military men who have assumed civilian clothes but retain a military mind, one that is accustomed to giving orders and having them followed. These idealistic young men set goals for reform and change which they genuinely wanted to achieve but which proved difficult of attainment and thus caused frustration. Rather than submit to criticism and public opinion, however, the young officers often preferred to consult only themselves or others like them. They see themselves as an elite corps that will guide and control the country from the top, while the masses of people follow. They have a great distrust and lack of faith in the masses whom they see as ignorant and in need of guidance. Their military mind carries over into the government, for they feel that the nation, whatever the costs, must be unified under one command and that all people must accept that command. Lip service is paid to democracy, but the officers are not true democrats.

They are likewise willing to repress and violate individual freedom if they feel it is necessary. We have seen how the Arab socialist theorist, Michael Aflaq, argued that Arab Socialist regimes, no matter what they did, would return inevitably to individual freedom, for such freedom was part of Arab tradition, and this tradition would act as a modifying influence on the excesses of absolutism and tyranny. This check on tyranny, however, has not yet appeared. Today in Iraq and Syria there is no respect for individual human rights and the situation is only somewhat better in Algeria or Egypt. It can be argued, and it has been argued in these pages, that such repression is often necessary for stability and order; yet it should be pointed out too that governments that use such repressive measures rarely cease to use them or give them up, repression and tyranny becoming part of the governmental structure. Perhaps the radical government should be reminded too that such repression violates the Koran, which urged compromise, discussion, and concord.

Another evil that afflicts the radical Arab World is bureaucracy. Even before socialism, governments hired large numbers of people to administer and manage the country. After socialism, these bureaucracies expanded rapidly as new agencies were established to deal with new government power. The radical regimes also used the bureaucracies to provide jobs for the unemployed. The end result has been enormous agencies that the countries can little afford; they are inefficient and disorganized, for they have grown too rapidly with too few trained personnel. They have also caused a rise in corruption, the element of Arab life the radical governments had otherwise so successfully confronted. Government administrators were becoming a new upper class with the best paid jobs in the nation and in control of the power structure. Nasser had recognized this in the late '60s and had taken steps to stop it. Yet there was little he could do; the agencies were needed to run the country, and he could not fire large numbers of people in a country already plagued by a shortage of jobs. In Algeria, because of the number of experienced French administrators advising the government, the problem is less pronounced. Yet even there, it has not been solved. Some method of limiting and controlling the bureaucracy has to be developed before the radical regimes become socialist states for the benefit of government employees, with all other citizens holding second-class status.

Finally, a last criticism that can be leveled at Arab Socialism is that it does not seem to have made much difference in practice. Tunisia, which has never adopted the radicalism and extremism of the Arab Socialist states, has achieved what is perhaps the most pronounced progress in the Arab World, by a cautious, deliberate program under the guidance of Habib Bourguiba. Conservative Arab governments are improving the lot of their citizens while remaining steadfastly traditional and stable. Beside the chaos, disorder, and upheaval that have characterized Arab radicalism, these regimes seem models of political maturity and achievement.

Yet it is doubtful that Egypt, Algeria, Syria, or Iraq could have imitated the Tunisian or any other model of political reform. Each of the radical nations faced problems of far greater magnitude than those facing other Arab countries. The conservative Arabs have oil to finance government and reform; they do not have minorities that divide and disrupt national unity. Oil-poor Tunisia is a small nation, whose struggle for independence against the French was not so bitter and destructive as Algeria's. In the radical nations, radical problems cried out for radical solutions, and Arab Socialism may well have been the only means to meet the crisis.

Arab Socialism has thus been one answer to the vicious circle that plagued the Middle East and prevented its modernization. It has not brought an end to poverty, ignorance, and human misery, but it has begun a concerted attack upon them. In looking at the Arab World, we must remember that these are a people who have only recently been awakened; it took centuries for the West to develop the responsible, humane governments that now characterize Europe and America. If we find Arab Socialism unappealing, we should remember that earlier forms of government in our own tradition—absolute monarchy, for instance—would be equally unappealing and repugnant. Arab Socialism is a current philosophy in the Arab Awakening; others will follow that will more adequately meet the needs and hopes of the Arab people, and perhaps one day will lead to that goal of unity that all the thinkers of the Arab Awakening, from the earliest to the most recent, have seen as important and desirable.

❧

Capsule Descriptions of the Arab World from West to East

Morocco. Area: 172,834 sq. mi., or somewhat larger than California. Population: 15,230,000. A French protectorate up to 1956. Primarily an agricultural country with cereals, vineyards, fruits, and dates as the most important products. Morocco leads the world in the amount of phosphate exports and has sizable cobalt deposits. There is a large tourism industry.

The ruler is King Hassan II. The monarchy is considered unstable but the king successfully put down an army revolt in 1971 and lived through an attempt on his life made by several air force pilots in 1972. Morocco supports the Arab war on Israel. Capital city: Rabat. Tangier and Casablanca are important cities.

Algeria. Area: 919,591 sq. mi., or larger than the United States east of the Mississippi River. Population: 15,000,000. Vast oil and natural gas deposits. Agriculture also important, with products such as olive oil, dates, and cattle among the most consequential. Significant deposits of iron, zinc, and other important minerals are also present. Tourism is growing in importance.

French and Arabic are the languages of the majority of people, but there are likewise sizable numbers of Berber tribesmen in the Atlas Mountains and the Sahara. The Berbers speak a language unrelated to Arabic and are descendants of the original inhabitants of North Africa. Capital: Algiers. Other cities: Constantine, Oran.

Tunisia. Area: 63,378 sq. mi., or somewhat larger than Michigan. Population: 5,100,000. Formerly French; independence gained in 1956. Primarily an agricultural country. Produces grains, dates, olives, figs, and vegetables. Livestock is also raised. Some mining of phosphates and iron; there is some oil. Tourism important.

Head of the government is Habib Bourguiba, a strong man who has guided Tunisia through moderate socialist reform. There is an elected National Assembly. Tunisia has taken a moderate stand on Israel, urging negotiation and compromise. Capital: Tunis.

Libya. Area: 679,358 sq. mi., or substantially larger than Alaska. Population: 2,010,000. Rich in oil. Some agricultural produce such as tomatoes, wheat, and barley, in addition to sheep and goats.

The conservative monarchy of Idris I was overthrown on September 1, 1969. Libya had been at one time an Italian colony. The new revolutionary government was under the leadership of Colonel Qaddafi, a devout Muslim, who declared that he would bring socialism and a restoration of Islamic piety to his country. Qaddafi has been loud in his denunciations of the West and of Israel. He has undertaken socialist reform in Libya. But he remains an unstable figure who has isolated himself from the other nations of the Arab World by his attacks on Sadat and King Hussein and other conservative Arab leaders. Capital: Tripoli.

Egypt. Area: 386,100 sq. mi., or more than twice as large as California. Population: 34,130,000. Coptic Christians comprise 7 percent of population; Muslims 92 percent. Oil present, but not in great quantities; new fields discovered in 1972. Cotton, sugar cane, and rice are important agricultural products. Capital: Cairo. Important cities: Alexandria, Asyut, Port Said, Suez, and Aswan.

The Sudan. Area: 967,500 sq. mi., or about the size of Alaska, Texas, and New Mexico combined. Population: 16,090,000. Arabs live in north; blacks in the south. Roughly 50 percent are Muslim, others are pagan, with small numbers of Christians.

Principal source of gum arabic for the world. Sorghum, cotton, peanuts, sheep, and camels are also important. Chrome ore is present, but the Sudan, despite its size, does not seem to be rich in minerals.

Former British colony; independence came in 1956. In 1969 a Revolutionary Council seized power; Gaafar al-Nimeiry is now president. Moderate reform has taken place, but the poverty and backwardness of the country make this reform of doubtful significance. Government has withstood an attempted communist coup and has made peace with the non-Arab rebels of the south who had carried on a war with the predominantly Arab government. Capital: Khartoum.

Jordan. Area: 37,500 sq. mi., or about the size of Indiana. Population: 2,380,000, a large number of which are Palestinian refugees who have fled Israel. A poor country with some agricultural produce such as tomatoes, wheat, citrus fruits, and olives. Mineral resources are few, except for raw phosphate, which is the country's leading export.

The ruler is King Hussein I. Jordan was created after World War I. It was a British mandate until after World War II. A supporter of the war against Israel, Jordan has nevertheless maintained a friendship with the United States. An unstable country; the king must balance the demands of his country's Palestinian refugees and the radical terrorist groups with his own more conservative Arabism. There have been several assassination attempts, but Hussein manages to survive the difficult situation. Capital: Amman.

Lebanon. Area: 4,015 sq. mi., or somewhat smaller than Connecticut. Population: 2,870,000. Lebanon is unique among Arab states in having a population half Christian and half Muslim. Primarily a trading nation (two-thirds of national income is from trade). Banking important and industry expanding. Some agricultural produce. Created from Ottoman Empire in 1920. French mandate until 1946.

President is elected for six-year term. He is to be a Christian, while the premier is a Muslim. An elected Assembly. Lebanon has had severe problems with Palestinian guerrillas who have used the country as a base to carry on war with Israel. The government attempts to follow a moderate course, trying to remain close to the West without unduly alienating the Arab World. Capital: Beirut. Important cities: Tripoli and Sidon.

Syria. Area: 72,234 sq. mi., or about the size of Missouri. Population: 6,500,000. Majority are Sunnite (Orthodox) Muslims, but there are sizable segments of smaller Islamic sects such as the Druze, the Alawites. A small Christian minority likewise exists. Chief products are agricultural, such as cotton, cereals, wool, and tobacco. Important oil pipeline from oil-rich Iraq to Syrian Mediterranean port cities supplies a great deal of revenue.

Formerly French; independence after World War II. A hard-liner against Israel. Capital: Damascus. Important cities: Latakia, Homs, Aleppo.

Iraq. Area: 173,259 sq. mi., or somewhat larger than California. Population: nearly 10,000,000. Muslim population divided between Orthodox and Shia sects; Iraq has the largest number of Shiites of any Arab nation, but the Shiites form an impoverished, uneducated segment of the population which is suspicious of the Orthodox Muslim segment. There is a vociferous Kurdish minority in the North that considers itself racially distinct from Arabs and demands recognition of its rights and privileges as a separate people. Iraq will be plagued by civil war and internal division for some time to come.

Economically, however, Iraq is potentially the most independent of the radical Arab lands. There is much oil—which provides 70 percent of the national income. But agriculture is also important. There are large herds of sheep, while wheat, barley, cotton, and tobacco are the chief crops.

A hardliner on Israel, Iraq has now turned its attention toward resolving conflicts with its neighbors to the east and south: Iran and Kuwait. Capital: Baghdad. Principal cities: Mosul, Kirkuk, Basra.

Kuwait. Area: 6,178 sq. mi., or about the size of Connecticut and Rhode Island. Population: 830,000. Formerly a British colony; became independent in 1961. This small country is extremely rich in oil, with about 15 percent of the world's known reserves (this is almost three times the oil reserves of the United States, including the Alaskan oil fields). Because of the oil, the people of Kuwait enjoy one of the world's highest per capita incomes. The government has established a welfare state that provides medical care, education, and social security for all citizens. Ruler: Emir Sabah al-Salim al-Sabah. Capital: Kuwait City.

Saudi Arabia. Area: 870,000 sq. mi., or about the size of the American Southwest, including Texas, New Mexico, Arizona, California, Nevada, and Utah. Extremely rich in oil, with about 7 percent of the world's annual output. Iron ore, gold, and silver have also been discovered. There is also an agricultural industry with dates, wheat, and wool, being the chief products.

Leadership of this conservative and deeply religious country is firmly in the hands of the Saudi dynasty. After the assassination of

King Faisal in March, 1975, Prince Khalid became king. The new ruler and his advisers are expected to maintain Faisal's close association with the West, while at the same time supporting the Arab struggle to limit and contain Israel. Saudi Arabia can be numbered among the world's wealthiest nations, and it will exert a steadily increasing influence in world affairs. Capital: Riyadh. The Islamic Holy Cities of Mecca and Medina are located in the country and annually draw great numbers of pilgrims.

Bahrain. Area: 231 sq. mi. Population: 220,000. British possession until 1971. An island nation with oil which has recently shown signs of running out. Some agricultural-related products, such as shrimp, pearls, and fruit. Ruler is Isa bin Sulman al-Khalifa. Capital: Manama.

Oman. Area: 82,000 sq. mi., or about the size of Idaho. Population: 680,000. Oil discovered in 1964 and now under development. Dates, goats, and limes are the main agricultural products. Ruler is Sultan Qabis bin Said, who has had some trouble with leftist guerrillas in the southern section of his country (near the border of southern Yemen). Capital: Muscat.

Qatar. Area: 6,000 sq. mi., or about the size of Hawaii. Population: 115,000. Formerly British; independence declared in 1971. Rich in oil; there is also some commercial fishing. Ruler is Emir Khalifa bin Hamad al-Thani, but there is also a prime minister and Council. Capital: Al Dawhah.

United Arab Emirates, also known as *Abu Dhabi.* Area: 32,278 sq. mi., or about the size of Maine. Population: 200,000. Formerly British; independent 1971. A union of seven sheikhdoms ranging in population from Dubai with 59,000 to Umm al Qaiwan with 3,700. Oil rich. Ruler is Zayed bin Sultan. Capital: Abu Dhabi.

Yemen Arab Republic. Area: 75,289 sq. mi., or about the size of Nebraska. Population: nearly 6,000,000. Economy is primarily agricultural with mocha coffee, cereals, dates, cotton, and herbs being the chief products. Some precious stones are mined.

A bloody civil war ended in 1970. There is now a coalition government with royalists and leftists both represented. The situation is unstable, with Saudi Arabia preserving peace and order. Capital: Sana.

People's Democratic Republic of Yemen (Southern Yemen).

Area: 112,000 sq. mi., or about the size of Arizona. Population: 1,500,000. A poor country with few known mineral or agricultural resources. Formerly the British colony of Aden; gained independence in 1967. A far leftist government is in power and maintains close ties with China, but because of the extreme backwardness and poverty of the country, Southern Yemen remains undeveloped and with little hope for the future. Capitals: Aden and Medina as-Shaab.

SUGGESTED READING

Anyone interested in Arab history and society should be aware of these four important and indispensable books: Morroe Berger, *The Arab World Today*, New York, Doubleday, 1962;* Manfred Halpern, *The Politics of Social Change*, Princeton, N.J., Princeton University Press, 1970;* Daniel Lerner, *The Passing of Traditional Society: Modernizing the Middle East*, Glencoe, Ill., The Free Press, 1964;* and J. C. Hurewitz, *Middle East Politics: The Military Dimension*, New York, Octagon, 1969.* Berger analyzes present-day Arab family life, the emancipation of women, the secularization of religion, and other problems of interest to a sociologist. Halpern concentrates on the political problems of the Middle East. Lerner deals with the impact of modernization on traditional society, while Hurewitz discusses the powerful role played by the military in all Arab nations. Each book contains an excellent bibliography for further research and reading.

For students interested in the origins of Islam and the early development of the Arab people, there is a good, short introduction in H. A. Gibb, *Mohammedanism: An Historical Survey*, London, Oxford University Press, 1953.* More detailed studies are offered by: P. K. Hitti, *History of the Arabs*, London, St. Martin, 1970, and Bernard Lewis, *The Arabs in History*, London, Harper & Row, 1950. The Koran has been translated by Mohammed Marmaduke Pickthall, *The Meaning of the Glorious Koran*, New York, New American Library, n.d.* Pickthall was an English convert to Islam. For geographic references see Norman J. G. Pounds and Robert C. Kingsbury, *An Atlas of Middle Eastern Affairs*, New York, Praeger, 1963,* and the *Oxford Regional Economic Atlas: The Middle East and North Africa*, New York, Oxford University Press, 1960. A useful textbook of Middle Eastern history is Sydney Nettleton Fisher, *The Middle East: A History*, New York, Knopf, 1968.

For the individual Arab countries discussed in this text see D. C. Gordon, *The Passing of French Algeria*, New York, Oxford University Press, 1966; John Haylock, *New Babylon: A Portrait of Iraq*, London, Collins, 1956; Patrick Seale, *The Struggle for Syria*, New York, Oxford University Press, 1965; and P. J. Vatikiotis, *The Modern History of Egypt*, New York, Praeger, 1969. Also very helpful are the Area Handbooks prepared by the Foreign Area Studies program of The American University, which are available from the U.S. Government Printing Office, Washington, D.C. There are handbooks on Iraq, Syria, Egypt, Algeria, and on other Arab nations.

Finally, the student should look into Colonel Nasser's own description of the Egyptian Rovolution in his *Egypt's Liberation: The Philosophy of the Revolution*, Buffalo: Economica Books, Smith, Keynes and Marshall, 1955,* and Anwar al-Sadat's *Revolt on the Nile*, New York, John Day, 1957. Other documents of radical Arab history are contained in George Lenczowski, editor, *The Political Awakening of the Middle East*, Englewood Cliffs, N.J., Prentice-Hall, a Spectrum Book, the Global History Series, 1970.* Miles Copeland, a former American agent active in the Middle East, gives an interesting picture of espionage and politics in the Arab World in *The Game of Nations, The Amorality of Power Politics*, New York, Simon & Schuster, 1969. Copeland knew Nasser. There are several biographies of Nasser in English, but each falls short of capturing the personality and greatness of that very complex man.

*Paperback edition.

INDEX

Abbas, Ferhat, 39, 82
Abdul Hamid, Sultan, 34–35
Abu Dhabi, 123
Aden. *See* People's Democratic Republic of Yemen
Al Afghani, Jamal al-Din, 31–32ff., 111
Al-Ahd, 35
Al-Alayili, Abdullah, 43, 46
Al-Assad, Hafiz. *See* Assad, Hafiz al-
Al-Atasi, Feisal, 98
Alawites, 97, 100
Al-Azhar, 32
Al-Azhar University, 71
Aflaq, Michael, 44–46, 59, 98–99, 111, 117
Africa, 57, 89
Agriculture. *See* Farmers; specific countries
Ahmed, Hocine Ait, 81
Al-Bakr, Ahmed Hassan, 107, 108
Al-Banna, Hassan, 40, 47, 48, 52
Al-Barzani, Mustafa, 110
Al-Bazzaz, Abd ar-Rahman, 108
Alexandria, 10, 12
Al-Fatat, 36, 36
Algeria, xi–xiii, 59, 74–75, 78–95, 112ff.; in Arab world today, 5–6ff.;

capsule description, 119; and historical roots of crisis, 24ff.; and national awakening, 33, 34, 39
Algiers, 10, 83, 85, 86
Al-Hourani, Akram, 98
Al-Husri, Sati, 43–44, 46
Al-Jadid, Salah. *See* Jadid, Salah al-
Al-Khalifa, Isa bin, 123
Allah, 18ff., 23, 28
Al-Moquani, Mohammad, 34
ALN, 82, 86
Al-Nimeiry, Gaafar, 120
Al-Sadat, Anwar. *See* Sadat, Anwar al-
Al-Said, Nuri, 39, 41, 59, 104–5
Al-Takriti, Sadda Hussein, 108
Amer, Abdul Hakim, 49, 50
American University of Beirut, 30
Americans. *See* United States and Americans
Amman, 4
Ancestry, Al-Alayili and, 43
Arab-Israeli wars. *See under* Israel
Arab Renaissance Party. *See* Baath Party
Arab Socialist Union, 66–67, 74, 98
Arabic, 29–31. *See also* Language
Architecture, 12
Arif, Abd ar-Rahman, 108

Index

Lawrence, T. E. (Lawrence of Arabia), 36
Lebanon, 29, 100, 102, 121
Lerner, Daniel, 13
Liberation Rally. *See* National Union
Libya, xii, 2, 11, 86, 120
Lice, 10
Literacy, 11. *See also* Education and schools
Literature and books, 30–31, 71

March Decrees (1963), 88
Marxism. *See* Communism and communists
Meany, George, 84
Mecca, 16–17
Medicine and health, 10, 68, 94, 109, 114
Medina, 17
Mediterranean, 8, 73, 76, 101
Mehmed III, 24
Military, 112, 116. *See also* specific countries
Mohammad (Prophet), xi, 15–18, 20, 21, 23–24, 31, 32, 44
Mohammad Abduh, 32ff.
Mohammad Ali, 30
Morocco, 89–90, 94, 119
Moses, 18
Movement for the Triumph of Democratic Liberties (MTLD), 80, 81
Movies, 71
MTLD, 80, 81
Muslim Brotherhood, 40, 47, 48, 51ff.
Muslims. *See* Islam
Mussolini, Benito, 41

Naguib, Mohammad, 50ff.
Napoleon, 113
Nasser, Gamal Abdel, 5, 34, 46, 49–61, 62, 63, 67, 69, 71ff., 86, 98ff., 105, 106, 112, 117; death, 75–76
National Bank of Egypt, 64
National Charter, 62–64, 66ff.
National Constitution of the Arabs, 43
National Liberation Army. *See* ALN
National Liberation Front. *See* FLN
National Party (Egypt), 34

National Progressive Front, 100
National Union, 53–54, 66, 67
Nationalism, 45. *See also* specific countries
Natural gas, 73, 91
Netherlands, 4
Newspapers, 71
Nile River, 8, 10, 58; Delta, 55–56, 73
Nixon, Richard M., 4, 76, 103
North African Star, 39
Nuqrashi (Egyptian prime minister), 47

October war. *See* Israel
Oil, 2, 4, 118; Algeria and, 89, 91, 93; Egypt and, 72, 73, 76, 77; Iraq and, 104, 109
Oman, 123
Operation Shoeshine Boys, 87
Oran, 81
Organisation Spéciale (OS), 81
Ottoman Empire. *See* Turks

Palestine, 3, 36 (*see also* Israel); guerrillas, 102, 103
Paris, 35
Peasants (farmers), 8–10, 25, 114. *See also* specific countries
People's Democratic Republic of Yemen, 123–24. *See also* Yemen
Philosophy of the Revolution, 50, 57
Plague, 10
Poetry, 22
Polygamy. *See* Women
Press, Egyptian, 64, 71
Protestant missionaries, 30

Qabis bin Said, Sultan, 123
Qaddafi, Colonel, 11, 120
Qata, 123

Radio Cairo, 59
Rahmadan, 18
Red Sea, 73, 76
Rida, Rashid, 32–33, 35, 40
Rolland, Romain, 44
Russia. *See* Soviet Union